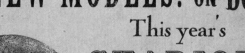

DEVIANT MOON TAROT™

BY PATRICK VALENZA

Published by
U.S. GAMES SYSTEMS, INC.

First Edition

10 9 8 7 6 5 4 3 2 1

Made in China

U.S. GAMES
SYSTEMS, INC

U.S. GAMES SYSTEMS, INC.
179 Ludlow Street
Stamford, CT 06902 USA
www.usgamesinc.com

Designed by Paula Palmer
Edited by Lynn Araujo

DEVIANT MOON TAROT™

TABLE OF CONTENTS

Acknowledgements and Dedications

This book is wholeheartedly dedicated to all the tarot friends I have made both online and in person since the deck's release. I humbly thank you all so much for supporting the Deviant Moon Tarot over the years and giving it a life I could never have imagined.

I wish to express my sincere gratitude to Stuart Kaplan for giving me the marvelous opportunities I once dreamed of as a boy. Special thanks to Lynn Araujo and Paula Palmer for providing their expertise and talents to help bring this immense project into reality. I would also like to thank my beautiful family for their love, understanding, and support.

As always, I want to thank H. Alan Feit, my friend and teacher, who first recognized and encouraged the artist within me, providing me with an artistic foundation fortified with commitment and dedication.

PREFACE

Writing this book was the biggest challenge of my creative life. Although I had never written anything of this magnitude before, I believed in myself and knew prior to starting that I would do whatever it took to accomplish such a task. One thing I underestimated was how long the book would take me to complete. When U.S. Games Systems first approached me to tell the stories behind the Deviant Moon Tarot, I figured the entire project would take no longer than three months. To my surprise, the manuscript took almost three years to write; nearly as long as it took to create the deck itself. During that time, I learned a great deal about myself, and I have grown tremendously.

The hardest thing to do was to consistently write whether I felt like it or not. In order to maintain my momentum, I habitually woke up in the middle of the night in order to work undisturbed in absolute silence. In those quiet hours, I heard the faint whispers of my muse as she fed the words I needed into my mind. More often, however, the words got stuck and I went for days without making any progress, which was terribly frustrating. With determination and persistence, the book finally came together, word by word. After living through this experience, I can now appreciate the struggle that writers go through, and I give them all enormous credit.

From an inspirational standpoint, the Deviant Moon Tarot has been at least thirty years in the making. This book chronicles my tarot journey, which spans from childhood into today. It is not only a testament to my art, but a record of my life. I hope something you find in the following pages inspires you to create a marvelous tarot deck of your own someday.

Patrick Valenza
Bellport, Long Island, N.Y.

Working hard in my pajamas at my drawing table, where the best ideas often came in the middle of the night.

"An Irate Magician" (1975, Age 8)

A Lifelong Journey

Most tarot enthusiasts have a personal story about how they discovered their first deck. Mine began in the mid-1970s when I was about nine years old. I was in a typical suburban shopping mall with my parents. The mall had an obscure corridor hidden at the end that resembled a French Tudor-styled village. I enjoyed walking around this dark and quaint section because it made me feel as if I was somehow going back through time. As my parents and I went inside one of the shops to browse, I caught sight of a small box of cards picturing the strangest medieval characters. It was love at first sight. I knew right then and there that I needed to possess whatever lay hidden inside that mystical cardboard box. Although I begged my parents to buy me a deck, I ended up leaving the store empty-handed that day. They could not see why a child needed to have a tarot deck. Despite their objections, I remained persistent.

After a few weeks, my parents gave in to my pleading and took me back to the mall to get my deck. I chose the one that I thought had the most interesting artwork, which I believe was the Swiss 1JJ Tarot. Elated, I ripped the box open before we even left the store. However, to

Making Paper Monsters (1972, Age 5)

my disappointment, I found that my new deck was in French. I adored the illustrations, but I also wanted to know the name of every mesmerizing character in the deck. We exchanged it for the less ornate Tarot Classic deck, which was in English so I could study it.

I could not have found the tarot at a better time in my life. I was young, full of imagination, and extremely intuitive. During those years, I had many strange dreams and premonitions. I also had dozens of vivid memories that I felt I'd been born with. These visions demanded to be expressed in some way or another. Tarot inevitably became my creative outlet.

I remember bringing my deck to school with me so I could give readings to my classmates in the schoolyard. While my friends were copying superheroes out of comic books, I was busy designing my own version of the Fool and the Magician. Out of this passion, I accidentally taught myself how to draw. I also used to write stories in my notebook about the Fool's misadventures in a supernatural land called Arcania.

Throughout my childhood, I made many attempts to create my own tarot deck. With each try, my designs evolved and my characters grew in detail. By the time I reached adolescence, my drawing skills were strong and I had an enormous amount of material to work with. I was finally ready to bring the deck I had envisioned in my dreams into reality.

Sumptuous Illuminations
The Original 13 Cards

Somewhere in my adolescence, I heard the term "sumptuous illuminations" used to describe iconic medieval paintings. These glowing words inspired me to try and create an original series of gothic-style altarpieces. While doing research for this new project, I came across photos of the beautiful Visconti-Sforza tarocchi cards painted in Italy during the mid-fifteenth century. Excited by this unexpected discovery, I abandoned the altarpieces and decided to paint a gilded tarot deck of my own instead.

The original 13 Deviant Moon cards were created between 1982-85 (age 15-18). They were made using acrylic washes on heavy watercolor paper. A light coat of metallic gold paint was applied to the background of each image, creating an ethereal glow. The elongated card dimensions were based on the Visconti-Sforza, measuring 4.5 by 7 inches. In keeping with my early altarpiece designs, I gave the cards arched, gothic borders fused with a bit of art nouveau styling. The border colors varied and were intuitively chosen by how well they complemented the color scheme of each individual painting. Various creatures or symbols decorated the top corners. At the time, I was unskilled in lettering, so I left the names and numbers of each card blank.

"Blue Moon Boy", unfinished section of an altarpiece (Circa 1981?)

My character stylization was influenced by ancient Greek art, yet I added a slightly abstracted twist. I chose to draw the full-bodied figures in a flat, playing card style, rendering them with heavy light and shadows, and then placing them against a shallow background. Although the figures are odd and distorted, they are also very human.

The moon has been a psychic friend to me throughout my entire life. As the sentinel of the night, it feeds my dreams and casts a strange glow on the way I see the colors of reality. Almost every drawing I have ever made shows the moon in some form or another. While creating the deck, the moon's influence over my imagination intensified, and the characters in the cards began to take on lunar traits of their own.

Although I intended to complete the Major Arcana, my artistic style was changing rapidly during those years, and it became difficult to keep the newer cards looking consistent with the previous ones. Before long, the cards faded out of favor and gave way to other creations. They eventually wound up stuffed inside a random book and were lost for more than a decade.

Rise of the Deviant Moon

As I moved into adulthood, my life became fraught with relentless distractions. Although I never stopped drawing and creating, I often had trouble staying focused on a single project long enough to complete it. I felt compelled to express my odd visions, yet I also wanted to pursue a career illustrating children's storybooks. When I worked on one aspect of my art, I felt guilty about neglecting the other. I went back and forth like this for years without accomplishing anything, or so it seemed. As a result of this indecision, I filled nearly one hundred sketchbooks with enough ideas to last a dozen lifetimes. I also packed several portfolio cases with a massive stockpile of abandoned drawings. These forsaken sketches and ideas would serve as an almost endless resource when it came time to work on the Deviant Moon Tarot.

I rediscovered the long-lost painted cards while going through my mother's belongings after she passed away in 2002. Having not seen them for years, the characters seemingly leapt out and recaptured my imagination. The deck was screaming for completion, but unfortunately, my procrastination caused me to mull over them for another two years.

Making a committed decision is the greatest thing one can do to change one's life. I made such a decision at the age of 37 onboard a train headed to New York City in 2004. I was with my family on a day trip thinking about life and how the years were moving faster than the view outside my window. In my younger years, I used to dream of going into Manhattan to show my illustrations to book publishers, but here I sat as a middle-aged man still without a portfolio to do so. I was getting older and had not yet brought any of my ideas to fruition or even showed my work to anyone outside my immediate family. I remember feeling overwhelmed by a sense of urgency because I did not want to take my ideas with me to the grave. The time had come for me to turn this situation around. Before our train reached Penn Station, I had made an unwavering vow to get busy and focus single-mindedly on one project until its completion. My first and only choice was to finish the tarot deck I had started in my youth.

CREATING THE DECK

Prior to restarting the deck in 2004, I had been experimenting with digital photo manipulations. I already had thousands of photos in my texture library; most of them of tombstones from the cemeteries I often visited. I had also begun exploring a nearby abandoned insane asylum, taking countless photos of its ruined architecture.

Instead of painting the cards as I did in my youth, I decided to use my photo collection to create the deck digitally. My first job was to remake the cards I already had. To do this, I simply scanned the old cards into the computer where I applied various photographic textures. I bent, twisted and reformed the tombstone photos to become the capes, boots, hats and robes worn by the Deviant Moon citizens. Using the photos I took from the insane asylum, I created all the background buildings pictured in the cards. Rotted doors, windows and walls became castles, factories and cities.

Gravestone photo manipulation (2003), left.

Sleeping soundly under a blanket of ice.

Springtime brings life into the garden once more.

PHOTOGRAPHIC SOURCES

THE CEMETERIES

The gravestone photos used in the Deviant Moon Tarot came from three sites. My favorite is the South End Burial Ground, which overlooks a small pond in East Hampton, Long Island. Here, the 18th century winged death head carvings remain in pristine condition. I come here often to do photo shoots or simply to find peace of mind.

Another one of my favorite sites is the enormous Green-Wood Cemetery in Brooklyn, New York. I first visited this necropolis midway through the deck's creation and spent countless days there taking thousands of photos of opulent mausoleums.

Luxurious housing for the dead.

Towering Gothic gates loom over all who enter.

The third site where I photographed textures was the Rose Family Cemetery in Brookhaven, Long Island. This is the eternal resting place of Scudder Ketchham, an American revolutionary war patriot who died in 1799. The grainy back of his crimson tombstone appears as a common texture throughout the entire deck.

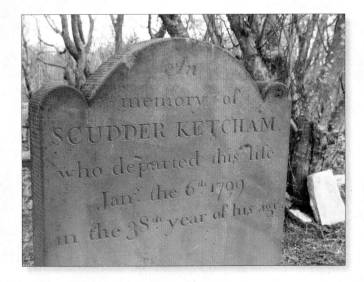

21

I have been fascinated by cemeteries for as long as I can remember. As a child, I used to explore the neighborhood churchyard with my best friend. We often snuck out of his bedroom window during sleepovers so we could roam the granite gardens under the moonlight. Our favorite spot was in the back of the graveyard, where we told ghost stories or tried to contact the dead. We loved reading the names on the tombstones, wondering about the long-gone lives of those sleeping below. Although we were just kids, we were always quiet and respectful. We even fixed knocked-over flowers left at gravesites, and occasionally picked up trash.

Every time my friend and I entered our cemetery, we gave a nod to the gatekeeper, whom we imagined was a spirit that stood watch over the residents inside. As long as we said hello to him, we felt welcomed. One time, my friend and I borrowed dirt from the gate area in order to practice a spell recipe we had gotten out of a library book. In exchange for the dirt, we left the gatekeeper a painted stone in its place. To this day, I still borrow a tiny sample of dirt from the gates of all the cemeteries I visit and put it in a glass bottle. As always, I leave the gatekeeper a generous gift in return.

Besides the painted stones, I sometimes pay tribute to the gatekeeper with an offering of a small clay head. I even leave whole figures on special occasions.

Gifts to the gatekeeper

Pilgrim State Asylum, N.Y.

Boogeyman Island

When I was very young, I often caught sight of a cluster of ominous buildings lurking in the distance as I sat in the back of the family car. I remember being awestruck by the towering black smokestacks that rose from the rooftops and penetrated the night sky. When I asked my mother about this place, she told me it was called Boogeyman Island. At that point, my imagination took over, wondering who lived there and what weird things they might be doing in the darkness. After telling my mother that one day I wanted to go there and look around, she replied by saying, "Those who go there never return." Her words did not discourage me; they only made me want to visit even more.

Unknown to me at the time, Boogeyman Island was in reality the Pilgrim State Psychiatric Hospital. Decades later, I wound up going there after all to visit a close relative in need of help. By that time, most of the site was in ruins. Though some areas were still functional, dozens of abandoned buildings lined the crumbling streets. I went on numerous expeditions photographing the outside of these decaying structures. These photos would go on to create an eerie world in which the Deviant Moon citizens could live.

In addition to the cemeteries and asylums, I also incorporated into the deck numerous photos taken from places across Long Island, New York. These photos range from parks and historic sites all the way down to an old wooden door at my former elementary school.

The main ward seems inviting.

The decrepit Pilgrim State power plant with its smokestacks amputated

Confronting Nightmares

When I was very young, I felt that I was sensitive to an unseen world beyond the veil of reality. Such feelings intensified at night, and often led to vivid nightmares. At times, I was acutely aware of a presence in my room, which I referred to as The Man. Although I encountered many nocturnal visitors during my childhood, this phantom was unlike any other. Whenever The Man appeared, thunder ripped through my mind and woke me up from a sound sleep. Knowing he was there was like looking at something from the corner of my eye; a formless blur without any details. I remember cowering under the blankets in terror until he was gone. Even during the day, I sometimes sensed The Man's peculiar energy all around me.

When I got a bit older, I decided to confront The Man after years of intimidation. During one of his nighttime visits, I defiantly rose from my bed and stood alone in the middle of my dark room waiting to have a word with him. When he failed to appear, I threw open my closet doors hoping to find him, but he was not inside. I then looked under my bed, but he was not there either. Frustrated, I turned on the light and continued searching my room. It suddenly dawned on me that I was stronger than my fears. I never saw The Man since or had another nightmare again.

"Abducted by the Man and Carried into the Night" (Age 8?)

"Trapped in a Lake of Fire" (1975, Age 8?)

On first impressions, the Deviant Moon Tarot may appear to some as a dark deck. However, in the following pages, you will find that this is hardly the case. This is a deck about self-empowerment. The Deviant Moon merely asks you to look within yourself and to face your fears. If some of the cards frighten you, it may be because you have a predisposed negative association in your mind to some aspect of the imagery. Know that you have the power to dissolve the shadows that haunt you whenever you choose.

Using This Book

I created the Deviant Moon Tarot intuitively. Many of the card images came to me fully finished in a flash of insight or in a lucid dream. While writing this book, I had to go back and examine the images in order to unlock their meanings. Since the deck's release in 2008, I have seen some incredible card interpretations from people all over the word.

Keep in mind that there are no rules when reading from this deck. Allow the images to pull insight from your subconscious. Because we all have different experiences and references in life, you may not see the same things that I, or other people, see in the cards. Use this companion book as a loose guide, and feel free to interpret the cards to suit your own unique psyche.

Major Arcana

0. The Fool

The Fool begins his journey with a delirious dance through the canal, leaving the conventional traditions of the city behind. With maniacal laughter, he heads out into the unknown, still clothed in his sleepwear. Half awake, half dreaming, the Fool treads water on the cusp of the conscious and subconscious realms, neither fully in one nor the other. A gondola waits in the background, which signifies the start of a voyage to self-understanding and enlightenment. Overhead, a crescent moon hangs in the sky. It serves as a beacon of subliminal influence that will follow the Fool wherever he goes. Although his nocturnal visions are entrancing, the Fool cannot totally escape reality. The fish from the canal nibble at his leg and keep him from falling too deeply asleep. Pointing to his head, the Fool reminds us that one's state of mind determines his path in life and that all great accomplishments start with a dream.

Upright meanings:

The Fool invites you to abandon all inhibitions and begin creating your own unique path through life, regardless of how far it deviates from the norm. Be receptive to wild, spontaneous notions, and allow your dreams to navigate your mind as you set out to explore your boundless potential. Seize the moment, and take a chance on yourself! Pursue your inspired visions, without waiting to gain competence or expertise first. Be advised that others may consider your improvised plans naive and your lack of preparation absurd. Have faith in your undiscovered abilities, knowing that you will soon learn all that is required along the way.

Reversed meanings:

When the Fool appears in a reversed position, he represents the loss of your inspiration. This can be attributed to a fear of the unknown, uncertainty in abilities, or the absence of imagination. It can also mean indecision or hesitation over new endeavors, as you may seek safe and tried solutions in an effort to avoid risk.

Harlequinade

As a child, I always felt that I was born with past-life memories. Visions of an insane harlequin dancing through a Venetian canal have always been a part of my childhood imagination. Back then, I desperately tried to express my thoughts by writing stories or drawing pictures. I also read countless books to try and find some historical reference to support my vision. When I discovered the tarot at age eight, I finally found something that connected to the strange characters running around in my mind.

During my childhood, I scribbled numerous variations of the Fool on the backs of index cards, napkins, paper bags, and on the margins of my school notebooks. Unfortunately, most of these drawings no longer exist. As the years went on, I refined my ideas while improving my style of drawing and character development.

Earliest surviving sketch of the Fool (Late 1970s)

Colored pencil (Circa 1981, Age 14)

Sketch (1982, Age 15)

Ink study (2010)

In my early twenties, I set off to design a totally new tarot deck unrelated to my childhood ideas; however, I only completed one painting for it. Something inside would not let me rest until I brought my original concept to fruition. It was as if a jealous spirit choked out and discouraged the creation of any deck that tried to take its place. Now that I have completed the Deviant Moon, I have surprisingly discovered the presence of several unique decks hidden within me, each begging to be expressed into a physical entity.

Early study (1980, Age 13)

The Fool (1988), left

I. The Magician

The novice magician performs onstage to the shadows of an imagined audience. Though he has not yet achieved mastery of skill, he envisions a time when he will be competent in his craft. His innate confidence lays for him a mental blueprint on how he can one day reach his goals. There is great effort and concentration expressed on his face as he wields the four symbols of the Minor Arcana. With time, practice and patience, he will become fluent in them all. Although the Magician has the inherent gift of four hands, he must still labor diligently to reach such a high level of craftsmanship. He dips his forefinger into a cup of blood, demonstrating that his art does not come without pain or sacrifice. The box at his knees is a material manifestation of the cosmos, symbolizing that mortals, as well as gods, can revel in the rewards of the universe through hard work, discipline and perseverance.

Upright meanings:

The Magician shows that you are more than able to master any desired skill through practice, sacrifice and a determined focus on your outcome. He encourages you to invest the time to cultivate your potential abilities. Occasionally, you may feel overwhelmed or frustrated. However, persistence to the task at hand will pay off. Stay confident in your craft, and believe that your creative power will manifest into tangible results. Be resourceful in your approach to all situations, remembering that you already have everything you need inside yourself to accomplish your dreams.

Reversed meanings:

The Magician reversed warns of the waste or misuse of your unique talents. There may be setbacks in undertakings due to uncoordinated efforts, and you might find yourself unable to grasp new concepts as confusion sets in. This could also signify the lack of confidence in your emerging abilities.

The Magician, colored pencil (Circa 1981)

Like the Fool, Venetian fashion influenced the design of the Magician. An early incarnation of his character appears in an illustration for a story I was writing in 1982. In the story, a mechanical fish made of gold arises from the canal and takes a few citizens on an exciting ride beneath the city. At the time, I was progressing in my work as a colored pencil artist, yet I was getting tired of drawing figures in a traditional manner. I felt the need to grow beyond what I was comfortable creating. When designing the Magician's body, I chose to combine abstraction with realism. Multiple arms came naturally for this figure, as it was a necessity for him to be performing with all four suit symbols. His stylized anatomy became the precursor to other odd body parts found throughout the deck.

Sketch (1982), left
"The Sinking City", colored pencil (1982, Age 15) pages 36-37

II. THE HIGH PRIESTESS

Surrounded by academic buildings and institutions, the High Priestess sits vigilantly on her pedestal, serving as the gatekeeper between man and supreme intelligence. Her bare feet are a sign of reverence for this sacred position. Crossing her arms, she guards the ancient knowledge contained deep within her soul. She is not always forthcoming with her wisdom, nor free with her information. She will only reveal her protected secrets to those who earn them. Regrettably, her beautiful wings are useless, for the dogma she has vowed to defend has hardened them into stone.

Spiritual imprints of past scholars adorn the Priestess's inner robe. This symbol represents the idea that all knowledge progresses off the advancements of others. The tip of her cloak has manifested into a snake, symbolizing mankind's temptation to use her knowledge for an evil purpose.

The High Priestess exists simultaneously in both a conscious and subconscious state. One side of her head resembles a crescent moon. This is where her practical knowledge, her accumulated facts, and her rationality reside. On her dark side, she receives infinite ideas from beyond in the form of a perpetual dream.

UPRIGHT MEANINGS:

Open your mind to the wisdom of the High Priestess! Like her, you can unlock your own intuitive knowledge and use it to enhance your overall cognitive power. By synthesizing both your conscious and subconscious thoughts, you will develop the ability to connect with divine intelligence. Unique solutions once hidden will suddenly be revealed as you gain profound insight into complex situations and deep mysteries. Remember, knowledge without application is worthless. It is not enough just to possess it. Take all that you learn in life and find a way to put it to good use.

REVERSED MEANINGS:

Ignorance is far from bliss! You may find yourself held back by unenlightened people who lack vision or imagination. Those around you act in secrecy and withhold the valuable information you require. The High Priestess in a reversed position may also signify the need to question established mores and reevaluate your own belief systems.

"Praying Priestess", early sketch (1983)

The stylized figures found on ancient Greek pottery influenced the appearance of the Deviant Moon citizens. As with Classical Greek art, my early characters were all flat faced; looking either to the left or to the right. I knew this profile view would get monotonous after 78 cards, so I began designing a frontal or quarter view that worked well with the flat figures I had already created.

The breakthrough I needed came when I remembered a painting I made when I was 12 years old. This old artwork depicted a blue angel with a divided face. She had one eye open and the other closed (see Temperance). After the evolution of a few sketches, I finally developed the double moon face seen throughout the deck. This innovation turned out to have a more symbolic and profound meaning later on as the cards progressed. It planted the idea of a dual conscious and subconscious state; half dreaming, half awake, balancing life along the thin line between imagination and reality.

THE MUTE LIBRARIAN

A dream I once had inspired the character of the High Priestess. In the dream, a winged nun dressed in a black cloak lived high atop a tall shelf in an old library. She worshiped silence, and she would throw books down at the children reading below if they so much as whispered.

Split Faced Priestess with Child (1983)

Moon Face Priestess (1983, Age 16)

III. The Empress

In her royal garden of thorns and pods, the young Empress sits in a pose of stately grandeur. A long, snakelike vine emanates from her body and wraps around her forearm. At the end of the vine, there is a large, orange bud ready to blossom.

The Empress is newly pregnant, and though the experience of motherhood has not yet occurred, she knows it will inevitably take place and change her life forever. Looking back over her shoulder, the Empress reflects over the carefree lifestyle she is about to leave, wondering if she is ready to put another's needs above her own. She questions if she will be competent to nurture her offspring. However, the gift of three breasts show that she is already adequately prepared.

Immaturity leads the Empress to internal conflict. As the vine coils around her arm, her mind struggles with the responsibility she is about to undertake. The claws on her feet wrestle for dominance over the growing umbilical vine in an attempt to stop its advancement. When the Empress realizes that the vine is a part of her, and not an outside invader, she will finally achieve peace within herself and embrace a more noble station in life than she could have possibly imagined.

Upright meanings:

The Empress personifies the nurturing role you must assume in order to bring your creative energy into its physical form. Allow the spirit of imagination to express itself through you, leaving all doubt and resistance behind. Keep your mind fertile, and tend to the needs of your mental garden. Have patience while you wait for your thoughts or ideas to be born into existence. Consider your brainchild as an extension of yourself, requiring careful cultivation to grow stronger. Be willing to make sacrifices for its benefit! By doing so, you will reap life's greatest rewards in abundance.

The Empress could also signify a changing life cycle or the anticipation you might have over an upcoming event. New ventures will depend on your support and cooperation. Come to terms with the responsibilities they bring. It is time to realize that you are capable of handling anything asked of you.

Reversed meanings:

Neglect has allowed weeds of negative energy to invade the gardens of your mind, spirit, and body. They choke out and prevent the growth of all creative endeavors. In this condition, your tangled inspiration will wither away, leaving you only with stillborn ideas.

Additionally, the Empress in reverse could suggest feelings of indifference towards one's responsibilities or duties. The flipped card could also be interpreted as the termination of a project before completion.

Early variations of the Empress (1982)

THE INSANE NURSERY

To accentuate their regal position in the Major Arcana, the Empress, High Priestess, Hierophant, and Emperor all sit on stone pedestals surrounded by a checkered tile floor. Inspiration for such flooring came from one of my earliest past life memories. The vision I have revolves around some curious events that occurred in a dark and dreary room, where I awaken to find myself hopelessly confined inside a caged crib. I know that I am a very young child, and I can hear the frightened cries of other unfortunate children in the distance. Misery and a sense of impending doom lurk in the shadows; however, there is nothing I can do to escape. Peering between the bars of my crib, I notice the checkered floor tiles below. The pattern leads my eye into the darkness beyond where I hear the sound of footsteps approaching quickly. The strange nightmare ends abruptly as someone reaches in and rips my hair apart. Although the tiles pictured in the four cards have nothing to do with this vision directly, they fulfill my desire to include elements of every uncanny notion I have ever experienced.

"The Insane Nursery" (Age 9?)

IV. The Emperor

The confident Emperor strikes a majestic pose and revels over his latest triumph. He proudly conveys his dominance through his regal staff, which he uses to pin a horrible demon down to the floor. The weight of his boot lends added physical assistance in keeping the beast at bay. The Emperor must be ever vigilant, however, or else the vanquished creature will try to escape and cause havoc in the city once again.

"The Knights Take the Offensive," early sketch (1982)

A small metallic moon has manifested into existence at the end of the Emperor's staff. This silvery crescent represents the transformation of his subconscious thoughts into a tangible form. Through vision, self-discipline and leadership, the Emperor has mastered his mind; and in turn, his world. He has become a potent and effective example to his people. Pointing his finger to his head, the Emperor shows us that true courage comes from the mind, not the heart. He waits in respite, yet this is only temporary. Powered by the momentum of his success, the Emperor looks to the future and his next conquest.

Upright meanings:

Take charge over your own mind! Like the Emperor, you must master yourself before you can control the outside world. Do not be afraid to harness the hidden powers of your subconscious. Use your intelligence to subdue any adversity that stands in the way of your ambitions. Thoughts alone, however, will not be enough to achieve your

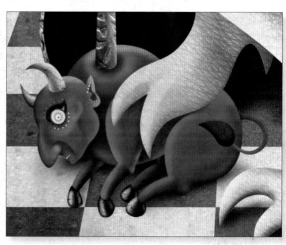

Close-up of the "Bull-Demon"

desires. You must turn your ideas into strong, determined action and boldly apply it toward your objective. Concentrate your mental energy into a clear purpose and lead yourself on to victory.

Reversed meanings:

The Emperor reversed is a sure sign of insecurity, indecision or incompetence. Mental concentration is unfocused, and you might find yourself unable to govern your own thoughts. Willpower is weak or impotent. Plans and ambitions fail due to inaction while a lack of self-confidence allows outside influences to dominate your life.

In an early design, a trio of miniature knights marches out from under the Emperor's robe to help defeat a treacherous red bull. (I later changed the bull's head into a demon's head for the final card).

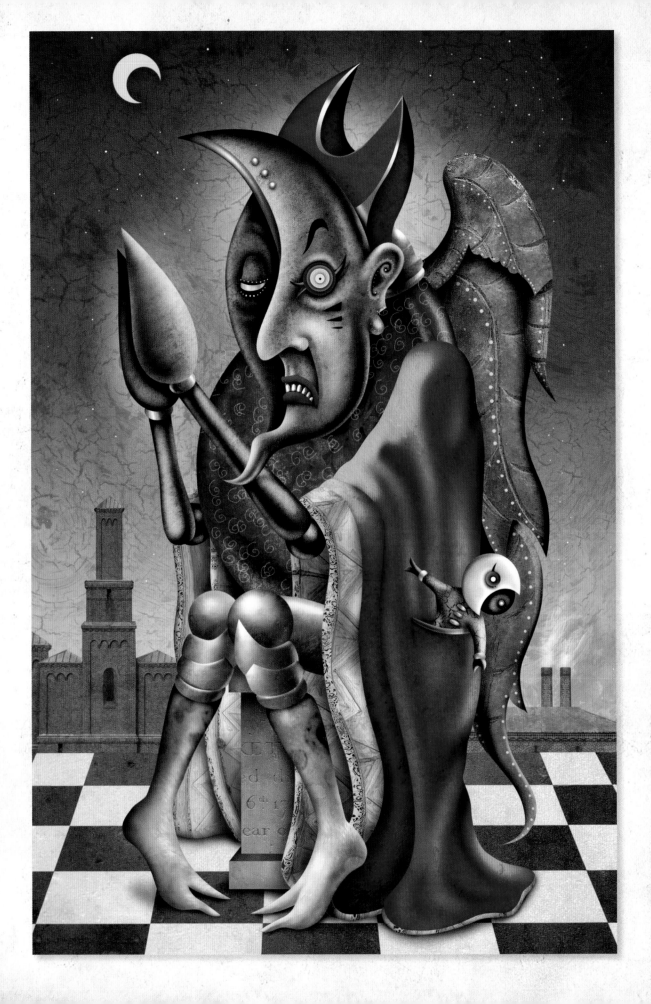

V. The Hierophant

Afraid to question his own convictions, the Hierophant prays not only for the souls of the city, but for his own, as well. What started for him as a journey towards spiritual enlightenment has only led to disillusion. Quivering with worry, he realizes that the doctrine he once so firmly believed in may not be the truth after all.

The Hierophant's sanctified life has become a constant struggle to maintain control over his faith and his flock. He projects fear into the thoughts of his congregation, holding their minds captive like the brainless doll ensnared in his pocket. The Hierophant derives his power from the false sense of spiritual security he bestows upon those who are unwilling to think for themselves. He deems those who question his teachings as unworthy and ostracizes them from his sacred circle.

The Hierophant suppresses the truth and turns joy into shame. His locked knees symbolize his close-mindedness and the apprehensive position he has towards sexuality. The conformity he preaches has petrified his wings and those of his followers, rendering all incapable of free flight.

Upright meanings:

The Hierophant represents an old philosophy that needs to be reexamined. Think for yourself and challenge outdated traditions! Any thought that limits your freedom or your happiness must be called into question. Fearlessly explore the established principals that have manipulated your life. Do not allow your mind to conform to the will of others. Now is the time to create and practice your own unique customs. Have faith in your personal convictions and be weary of those who try to impose their own beliefs upon you. Break free from the group and find the truth in yourself!

Reversed meanings:

A conflict may arise over an established tradition, causing anxiety and turmoil. You might find yourself unable to break free from the powerful grip of your old beliefs. Superstition and fear cloud your thoughts, leaving you unwilling to challenge the norm. You may also have difficulty changing the ritualistic paths embedded in your mind. Bad habits seem insurmountable.

"Three Wise Men", doodle in a school notebook (1983)

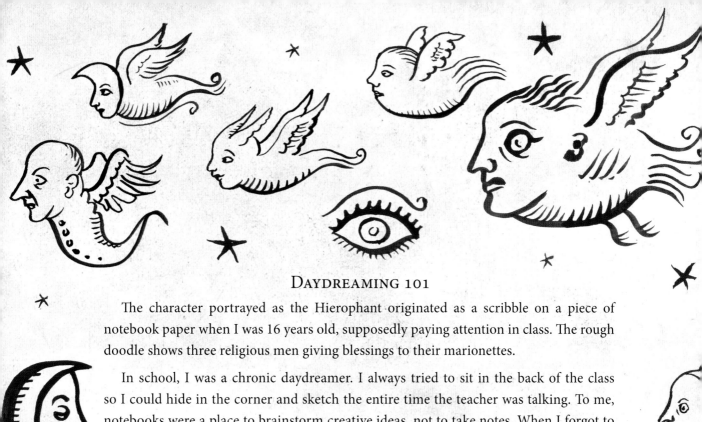

DAYDREAMING 101

The character portrayed as the Hierophant originated as a scribble on a piece of notebook paper when I was 16 years old, supposedly paying attention in class. The rough doodle shows three religious men giving blessings to their marionettes.

In school, I was a chronic daydreamer. I always tried to sit in the back of the class so I could hide in the corner and sketch the entire time the teacher was talking. To me, notebooks were a place to brainstorm creative ideas, not to take notes. When I forgot to bring a notebook to class, I would just simply draw all over the desk. On one occasion, my Math teacher walked by my desk and caught me in action. I thought for sure I would be in big trouble! He had a look at the poor desk covered in scribbles, then looked at me and said, 'Please continue.' He then gave me exclusive permission to draw on the desk for the remainder of the year. I did not hesitate to take him up on his offer.

VI. THE LOVERS

Locked in the grips of passion, two lovers press their bodies together on the shore of a desert lake. Attracted by one another's differences, they join as one united soul. Each fulfills the needs and desires of the other, sharing both positive and negative attributes. The female plays the emotional role in this symbiotic relationship. We see that her hair leads the viewer's eye into the water, indicating her deep subconscious thoughts.

The physical aspects of this relationship drive the male. His eye is wide and awake as he holds the woman possessively in his arms and kisses her neck. Barren desert mountains in the background warn him that if he bases his relationship on passion alone, it will be empty and void.

The moon above casts its hypnotic spell upon the pair, influencing all rational thought. Below, a snake bites into the man's leg, injecting him with intoxicating venom. Being so involved in the moment, he does not feel the sting. Soon, the seductive poisons will circulate through both bodies, rendering the pair unable to resist love's temptations.

UPRIGHT MEANINGS:

When the Lovers appear in a reading, they represent the dynamic power of two distinct forces coming together in harmony. Contrasting elements will merge, forming a new and unique entity. The card may also symbolize the need to bring your masculine and female energies into balance.

Additionally, the Lovers could mean that an intimate relationship will likely prosper. Love will flourish, and rapidly bloom into a heated romance. Furthermore, the card could be advising you to embrace the differences between you and your partner.

REVERSED MEANINGS:

When reversed, the Lovers signify that forces will likely repel each other rather than attract! Vibrations will not match, and synchronization will be off. Be forewarned of an impending split in a relationship. In this position, the card may also indicate unison for the wrong reasons, which will inevitably give way to conflict.

Like most of the characters in the Deviant Moon Tarot, the female pictured on the Lovers card originated in my teenage artwork. Back then, I made many drawings featuring a playful breed of bald, nude, marionette-like women. These women can also be found in such cards as the Three of Cups, Eight of Swords, Five of Pentacles and the Ace of Cups. The girl in the Lovers, however, is the only one of this kind to have long braids of hair.

"Puppet Show", white pastel (1984, Age 17), left

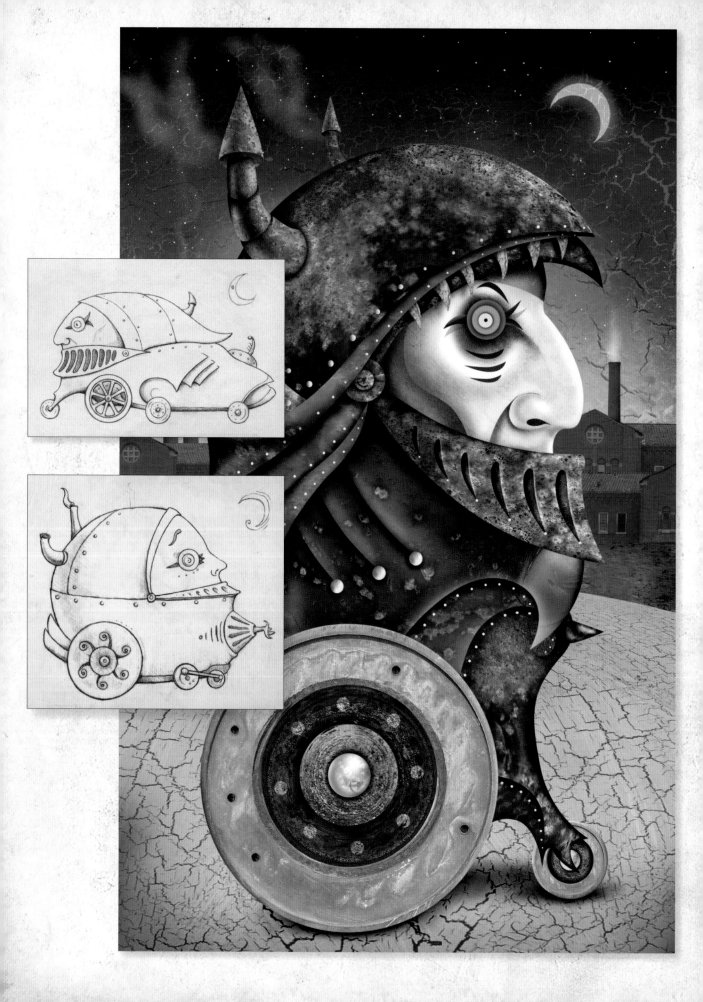

VII. The Chariot

Alone in a factory courtyard, the Chariot prepares to break free of his debilitating confines. No longer does he see himself as a helpless being lacking able limbs. He has changed his notion of what is possible through a powerful and resourceful mind. From this day forward, he will strive to achieve greatness and realize his own neglected potential.

The Chariot has fashioned his adversities into an armor of confidence, which proudly bears the scars of the mental battle he has waged over the years. His enlarged head shows that he has transformed himself into a warrior of tremendous will. It overflows with ideas that lead him into bold and immediate action. Although his eyes are weary, he keeps his thoughts focused on his destiny. Passion burns within his soul, giving him the energy he needs to propel himself into a well-deserved and bright future.

Rusted bicycle bell

Upright meanings:

The Chariot shows that you can overcome any hardship through a directed and determined mind. Concentrate on your desired outcome, and prepare for the battle of your life. Defy the limit you place upon yourself and others. Do not let excuses hold you back any longer. Remember, you will never be beaten if you never give up! Be resourceful and do whatever is necessary to fulfill your dreams. Free your imagination, and use it to form a viable plan. Take the initiative, build unstoppable momentum, and move yourself forward in a new direction.

Drainage hole

Reversed meanings:

Rust builds on the wheels of your life. The Chariot reversed exposes procrastination and self-sabotage. Doubt in your abilities leaves you constrained to dismal conditions. Perhaps you are allowing a physical or mental limitation to control your fate. In addition, you may have lost all motivation because you fixate on failure rather than success.

Old motor

Spare Parts

I created the Chariot in 2006. It was the first new addition to the deck since the 13 original hand-painted cards. However, it still had its roots in older drawings from years past. The inspiration for its creation came from some of the mind-powered mechanical vehicles that raced around the pages of my old, teenage sketchbooks. Each of these little sketches yearned to be dusted off and reworked into the character found on the current card.

Textures for the Chariot came from a few non-exotic sources. I constructed the vehicle entirely from three photographs: a rusted bicycle bell, a drainage hole, and a close up of an old car motor. These were all digitally manipulated to form the corroded armor and wheels.

Mind-powered chariots (Circa 1985), inset left

VIII. Justice

A powerful Judge holds two identical swords in perfect balance, delivering justice to all citizens. He serves the people without bias, and his decisive rulings are always impartial. Behind him, the moon rests quietly in the distant sky, indicating that emotions have little impact over his findings. The Judge looks directly at the viewer with straightforward honesty. His resolute gaze penetrates lies and exposes the truth. Because of his impeccable character, the city has granted the trusted judge complete access into its affairs. This stewardship is illustrated by the ring of keys he carries and the small keyhole seen on the background building.

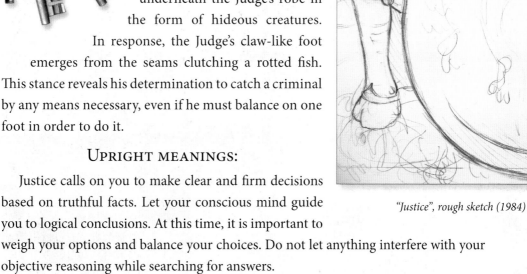

In his wisdom, the Judge realizes that what is justice for some may be an injustice to others. Despite his tireless efforts to keep society balanced, discrimination and corruption will always exist. Such iniquities slither out from underneath the Judge's robe in the form of hideous creatures. In response, the Judge's claw-like foot emerges from the seams clutching a rotted fish. This stance reveals his determination to catch a criminal by any means necessary, even if he must balance on one foot in order to do it.

Upright meanings:

Justice calls on you to make clear and firm decisions based on truthful facts. Let your conscious mind guide you to logical conclusions. At this time, it is important to weigh your options and balance your choices. Do not let anything interfere with your objective reasoning while searching for answers.

"Justice", rough sketch (1984)

The Justice card may be advising you to assume complete responsibility for your actions. Do not make matters worse than they need to be. Know that you must do what is morally right, regardless of the consequences.

Additionally, the card could refer to legal issues that you must attend to. Contracts need to be carefully evaluated. Judgments will turn out favorable if so deserved.

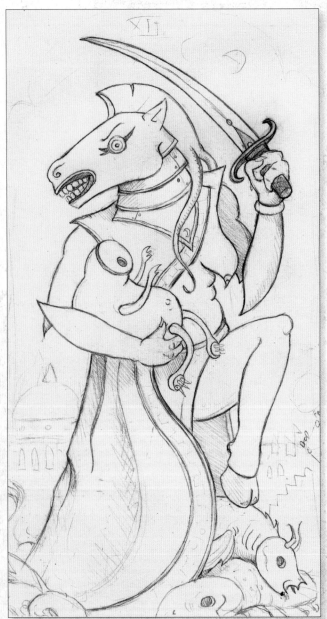

Preliminary sketch (1985)

Ruined card (1985)

When Justice shows itself in reverse, it can signify acts of moral turpitude and duplicity. The card could also signify a rash decision or a poor choice. Perhaps someone you know is using a past injustice as an excuse for immobilizing himself. In this position, Justice could also warn of legal troubles or unfavorable verdicts.

- Most modern decks number Justice as 11 and Strength as number eight. However, for the Deviant Moon, I have switched the numbers back to the traditions of the Marseilles and other pre-20th century decks. Since the Deviant Moon Tarot has no association to astrology or the zodiac, there was never a need to follow the numbering system imposed by the Rider-Waite deck.

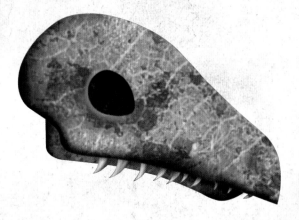

JUSTICE AND THE INFANT ARTIST

Out of the 13 original hand-painted Deviant Moon cards made in my teens, Justice was to be number 14. The early version pictured a horse-headed heroine defending a baby from the evils of the world. On the day I started working on the card, my younger sister had some friends over to play. One of them was a mischievous toddler, who decided to improve the artwork with some black paint while I left to take a break. Unfortunately, I did not have the motivation to remake the ruined card. After that incident, I stopped working on the hand-painted deck and moved on to other projects. My creative style was changing, and my ambitions switched to illustrating children's books instead.

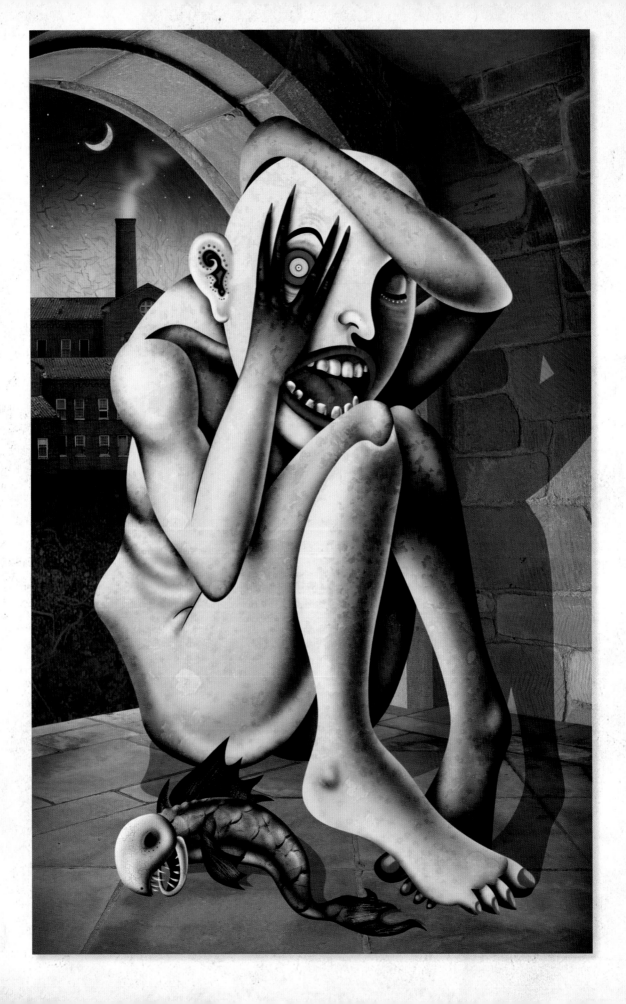

IX. The Hermit

Unable to cope with the stress and turmoil in his daily life, the Hermit makes a desperate attempt to hide himself away in an alcove. Taking on a fetal position, he huddles in terror, naked and vulnerable. His shivering body casts an enlarged shadow against the wall, magnifying the overbearing fear that dominates his wretched heart. His arm wraps around his head, binding and restricting all thoughts that could empower him. Through blackened fingers, his open eye peers out in anguish as he tries to awaken from this nightmare. He shuts the other eye tight, hoping to shield himself from a tormented reality.

The Hermit has turned his back on society; however, his self-imposed exile is imperfect. His hiding spot has no door, making it impossible to stop the winds of the outside world from whispering along his spine. At his feet lies a decomposed fish, reeking with the stench of anxiety. It serves as a stark reminder that one can never hide from himself.

Upright meanings:

When the Hermit appears in a Deviant Moon reading, it could mean that you are allowing fear to drive you into a corner. You may feel an urgent need to withdraw from your problems and disassociate yourself from the world's pressures. Know that your internalized fears will continue to stalk you until you courageously confront them, face to face. The Hermit might also represent feelings of extreme loneliness and isolation. In addition, he could personify a social outcast.

A lighter interpretation of the card could simply mean that you need time to be alone. Turn away from life's demands and find a quiet place to meditate in solitude. When you emerge from your peaceful retreat, you will undoubtedly feel refreshed, recharged and enlightened.

Reversed meanings:

In reverse, the Hermit affirms that you have the power within yourself to overcome your debilitating fears. By redirecting your thoughts, you will regain control over your mind as well as your circumstances. It's time to get back into life! Hibernation will come to an end, and you will renew social bonds.

APPARITION ON A SPIRAL STAIRCASE

The character of the Hermit came to me one night in a vivid dream. In this vision, I saw a filthy, little blue man cowering under a small archway overlooking a winding spiral staircase. He was hiding from the phantom shadow of an old woman climbing slowly up the stairs. As the apparition got closer to the blue man, her melancholy whispers grew louder until they echoed throughout the hall like thunder. I awoke in the middle of the dream and quickly sketched as much as I could remember.

The next day, I transformed my dream into a large artwork, using cut up pieces of painted paper, which I assembled into a gigantic collage. Sadly, the creation physically fell apart over the years. All that remains today is the little blue man, which found refuge inside one of my sketchbooks. To get him to fit safely inside, I regrettably cut off his feet along with his beautifully polished toenails.

The photographic source for the Hermit's alcove came from Coe Hall at the Planting Fields Arboretum, Oyster Bay, New York.

Paper cut-outs, acrylic washes (1985), left

63

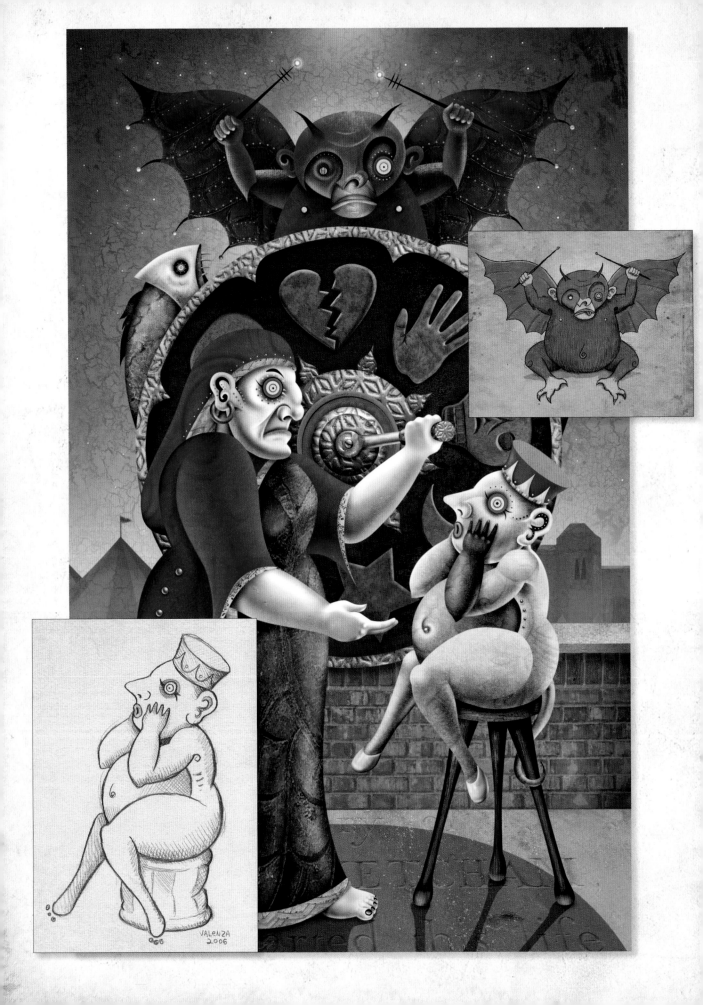

X. The Wheel of Fortune

Looking into the future with a blank stare, a sideshow gypsy prepares to spin the Wheel of Fortune for an uneasy customer. With her hand held out, she awaits payment, for there is always a cost when fate reveals her mysteries. The anxious customer relies on chance and the hope of good fortune to steer him through life. He sits on a wobbly old stool; a sure indication that the faith he has in himself may not be very sturdy.

Strange and powerful forces guide the revolution of the wheel. Appearing above, a winged monkey conjures the unknown secrets of the universe. One must watch the monkey carefully, however, since he is prone to mischief and could tamper with the results of fate's revelations. Two blind fish decorate the sides of the wheel, each headed in opposite directions. Like the customer, they allow the random spin of chance to dictate their course through the stream of life.

Upright meanings:

The Wheel of Fortune symbolizes the ever-spinning rotation of luck and misfortune. Both are simply inevitable occurrences in the cycle of life. Although each will appear and leave you at times, you must do all you can to create your own destiny. Refuse to become a victim of circumstance. Seize every opportunity that goes by and learn something valuable from every adversity. Gamble on yourself, and spin the Wheel of Fortune in the direction of your choice!

When this card whirls into your reading, it may also mean that you will soon experience an uncanny turn of events. Life might suddenly change, either for better or for worse. Know there is no way to predict the outcome. Expect the unexpected!

Reversed meanings:

In a reversed position, the Wheel of Fortune could indicate that your superstitious beliefs are leading you in the wrong direction. In your mind, the future seems predetermined with little hope for change. With such a negative outlook, you will only self-fulfill your own prophecies. Regrettably, you often wait around for good luck to improve your situation, while using bad luck as an excuse for not overcoming your hardships.

Fateful Mementos

My sketchbooks serve as illustrated diaries. At the end of every entry, I sign off by drawing several lucky charms. Over the years, these charms have developed to include such symbols as broken hearts, stars, moons, eyeballs, handprints, knives, and winged skulls. Each came to me intuitively, and their meanings remain locked in my wordless subconscious. I can only say that they somehow represent a few of my favorite things. It was only natural for me to incorporate these charms into the design of the Wheel of Fortune.

"Naughty Monkey", early ink sketch, (2006), top right inset
"The Dupe", sketch, (2006), bottom left inset

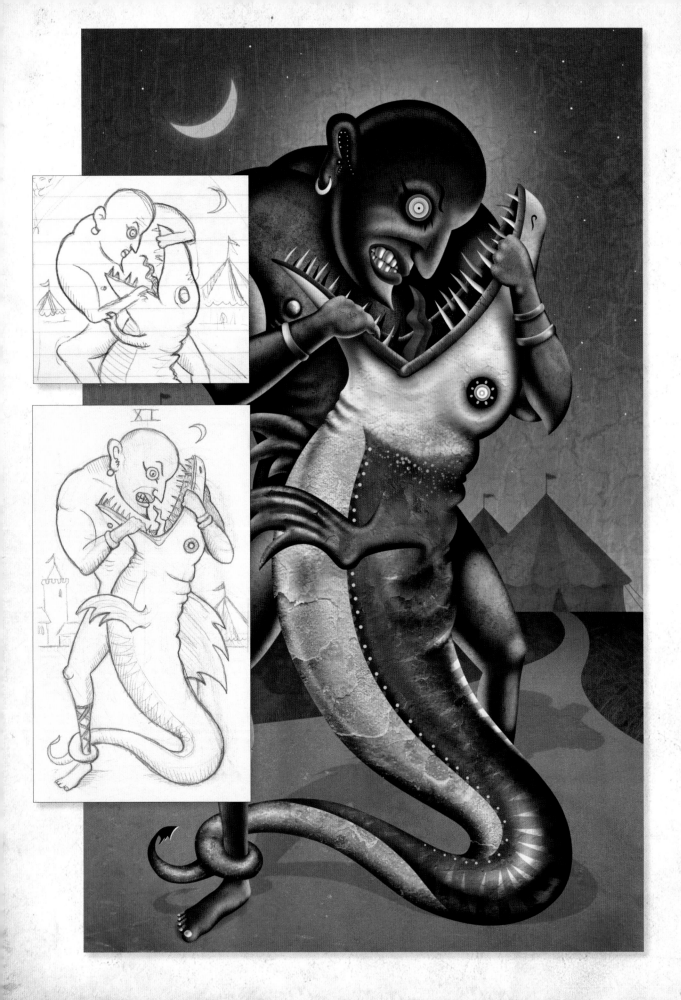

XI. Strength

With mental strength derived from confidence, a mighty wrestler exerts physical force over an untamed beast. Disregarding the danger, he pries the creature's jaws wide open, placing his head precariously close to its razor sharp teeth. He has accomplished this feat many times before, and experience has made him sure of the things he can achieve through practice and a determined mind.

Throughout the struggle, the wrestler must maintain his focus and concentration. Likewise, he must not become overconfident or arrogant, for the beast he dares to overpower will not succumb so willingly. It too fights for domination, and has curled its tail around the man's ankle in an attempt to throw him off balance. If he begins to doubt himself, the wrestler could be devoured in an instant. Certainty in his own abilities will allow him to triumph over this daunting situation.

Upright meanings:

When Strength appears in your reading, it advises you to combine your mental and physical energies into one indomitable force. Once this happens, you will have the power to endure any ordeal. Like a muscle, you will expand by courageously dealing with the demands life places on you. Always show bravery in the face of fear. Refuse to let adversity get the best of you.

In addition, the card may be challenging you to take control of your inner demons. By gaining the upper hand, you will be better able to cope with the troubles of the outside world.

Reversed meanings:

When Strength appears upside down, it tells of vulnerability and weakness. Your mind has become fragile, and your body has followed suit. Low energy leaves you incapable of concentration. Small tasks seem like an unbearable struggle. Fear cripples your confidence while insecurity wraps itself around your ambitions. While you are in this diminished state, your negative thoughts may overwhelm you.

Death at the Circus

I have an odd memory, one I have always attributed to a past life. I see myself as a young boy, maybe ten years old. I am at a circus sitting in the stands with my family watching the show. As my eyes roam, I spot some animals behind a curtain and quietly decide to sneak off to get a closer look. No one seems to notice me as I crawl underneath the drapery. In the shadows, I see a poor creature pacing back and forth in its cage. I am there for only a minute before I feel a hard crash on the back of my head. The vision ends abruptly right there. I do not know if someone clobbered me for trespassing, or if something fell on me. Either way, I know I died that day. The circus tent found in the background of the Strength card is a tribute to that strange memory.

"Strength", pen doodle in school notebook (1983, Age 16), inset top left
Early pencil sketch (1983, Age 16), inset bottom left

XII. The Hanged Man

Alternate concept sketch (Date unknown)

With an ankle bound by rope, a young man hangs upside down with his hands behind his back. It is unknown if someone has tied his hands, or if he places them there apathetically. In either case, they represent unused potential that might be better applied in the construction of a dynamic future.

The man's inverted reality drains all proactive notions from his mind. Though he often thinks of what he should be accomplishing right now, there is no urgency from within to act upon his dreams. Time steadily and relentlessly slips away as he dangles in a static state of limbo.

The Hanged Man is complacent in his stagnation, and he allows life's opportunities to pass by like the breeze. His crossed leg implies that he is filled with indecision and internal conflict. Even so, he does not struggle or attempt escape. He wears the finest of clothing and appears to be well nourished. Comfort has immobilized his ambitions and removed his desire to liberate himself from his wooden post. Only when his current setting becomes too agonizing to endure will he muster the conviction to break free of its restraints.

Upright meanings:

When the Hanged Man swings into your reading, he personifies your suspended ambitions. Regrettably, you might have become lazy in the pursuit of your dreams. Perhaps your need to feel secure is preventing you from taking a risk and achieving success. Stop lingering around hoping for inspiration to come move you into action. Know that you will stay in one place forever unless you decide to cut the ropes fashioned by fear. It is worth the effort to struggle for a better position in life. Do not postpone your future any longer, the day you have been waiting for is here right now!

Reversed meanings:

In a reversed position, the Hanged Man is obviously no longer upside down! He seems to float in the air like a balloon on a string. Gravity no longer applies, and time comes to a standstill. This metaphor represents stalled advancement in your life. Progress grinds to a halt, causing an inconvenient pause in your momentum. You may find yourself getting caught in circumstances, internal or external, that delay your plans and hinder your aspirations.

In addition to his pocket watch, the hourglass shape of the Hanged Man's torso subtly suggests the notion of time.

Sketch (1984, Age 17), inset left

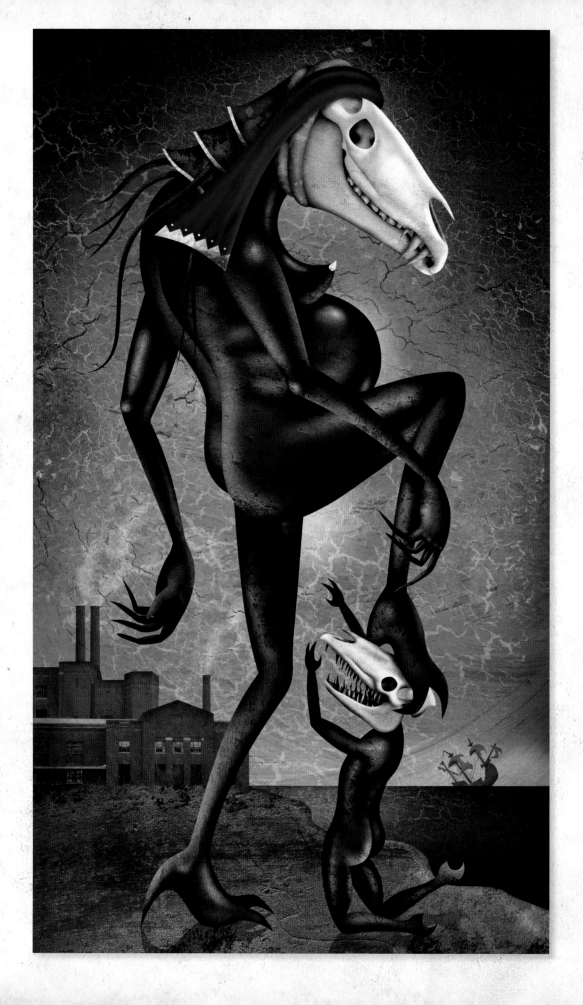

XIII. DEATH

Under a moonless sky, the macabre corpses of a mother and child stand ominously along a contaminated shoreline. The horrific sight of their decomposed bodies can cause the hearts of even the bravest men to shrivel with fear. Once alive and vibrant, their lethal environment has changed them into toxic cadavers. Pollution from the factories has laid the land around them to waste and blackened the sea. On the horizon, a doomed sailing vessel sinks beneath the poisonous waves; all souls are lost.

The mother's eyeless skull faces the future, suggesting that life will continue despite the vile conditions of the present moment. Her child turns to the past, looking to escape this lurid dream. Pleading on his knees, he tries to reenter the womb of his dead mother, who prevents him from doing so with the claws of her rotten foot. Once born, there is no return. Like his mother, the child must accept the circumstances set before him and move on in search of better days. Although the mother is the incarnation of death itself, she also bears the seed of new life. Soon, the birth of another child will take place, bringing with it the hope of regeneration.

UPRIGHT MEANINGS:

The Death card marks the abrupt conclusion of one aspect of life and the start of another. Know that death is not the end, but merely the point of transition within a cycle of continuous change. It marks the perpetual transference of energy from one form of existence into another. Have no fear of your metamorphosis! Accept that this change is inevitable and permanent. There is no going back to the way things were.

Though your situation may appear grim, feel at ease. Good things are waiting to emerge from bad situations. New creations will arise from decay, and revitalize what has been ruined. All that is old will soon be swept away, clearing the path for new and promising beginnings.

REVERSED MEANINGS:

When reversed, the Death card forewarns of turbulent change brought about by unfortunate situations. Mental upheaval might possibly come as the result of a traumatic experience, or a sudden life-altering event could cause you to suffer great loss. You may be facing this unwanted transition with denial or resistance. Fear of an unknown future leaves you incapable of progress.

Death, also known as Trump XIII, appears in the Deviant Moon Tarot as an unnamed card. This goes back to the traditions of early decks like the Tarot de Marseille (1600s). In a time of widespread superstitions, people considered it unlucky to utter Death's name aloud. They simply identified the card by the skeleton or the number 13.

My teenage sketches for 'Death' involved a creature with a bird's skull for a head. Dressed like a jester, he played an out-of-tune mandolin to a group of young maidens. As ideas

Early version of Death (1985)

"*Skeleton Mother & Child*" *(1975, Age 8)*

evolved, I settled into a more profound concept; life replenished through new births. In order to express this idea, I changed the Death character into a pregnant corpse.

DEATHMARE

When I restarted the deck in 2004, I replaced the original bird skull with one from a horse. The idea to do this came to me in a chilling dream, where I saw a skeletal horse trotting through the streets of an old city. The putrid beast was an omen of death, and it brought misery to all it passed. Citizens hid fearfully inside their homes when they heard the horse's bony hoofs clicking down the alleyway. If the prophetic horse should stop at your door, it was a sure sign that some unfortunate person in the house was to die quite soon.

The Omen of Death

Ink sketch (2004)

XIV. TEMPERANCE

The Angel of Temperance has flown over desolate mountains in order to gather water from a tranquil oasis. Here she pauses, half dreaming on the edge of sub-consciousness. Creative energy fills her body as she taps into the inspirational resources surrounding her. The tips of her toes touch the surface of the water, connecting her spirit to limitless imagination while her pinky finger points to the heavens, demonstrating an effortless ability to channel divine guidance from above.

Isolated from the distractions of the city, the Angel begins to quiet her mind. Her blue skin is a reflection of her peaceful demeanor. With calm focus, she draws water from the oasis and patiently mixes it with her urns. Time flows as she pours the liquid back and forth. Memories of the past combine with the hopes of the future to create the ever-changing essence of the present moment. Although the vessels she uses are of contrasting design, her ingenuity enables her to concoct a potion of balance and harmony. When she achieves the perfect blend, the Angel will fly back to the city and deliver this unique elixir to all thirsty citizens.

UPRIGHT MEANINGS:

When Temperance appears in a reading, it suggests that you synthesize diverse thoughts into new and powerful ideas. Now is the time to bring opposites together for a common purpose. By mixing creativity into your efforts, you will achieve the unique results others have only dreamed of! Concentrate fully on the task at hand and utilize your natural ability to do the impossible.

Like the Angel of Temperance, you must retreat from the demands of the world in order to work on your vision. Open your mind to a higher state of awareness through silent meditation. Furthermore, Temperance advises that you do whatever is necessary to correct the imbalances in your life. Look for inventive ways to rejuvenate your spirit and heal your body.

REVERSED MEANINGS:

When Temperance appears in reverse, the card indicates conflict, discord, or other unbalanced aspects of your life. Bad combinations and an overall lack of cooperation will yield inconsistent results. You could be trying to force a situation without giving it the time needed to develop properly. Interruptions from the outside world will invade your thoughts and drain the creativity from your mind. Misuse of mental energy and wasted resources may leave you uninspired or unable to connect with your imagination.

THE BLUE ANGEL

When I was 12 years old, I painted the portrait of a praying blue angel on a day when I was home sick from school, yet filled with creative energy. Although I had never painted anything before, I was curious to experiment with some unused art supplies gathering dust on top of a cabinet. With no plan on what I was going to make, I simply improvised and allowed my intuition to guide the paint across the canvas. Before long, I ended up with a blue moon-faced figure.

While painting the eyes of this strange character, I worried that I would not be able to make one look just like the other. As I slowed down to think, I noticed that his unfinished eye appeared to be winking. Believing I might ruin my work if I continued, I left him this way, deciding in my imagination that he would be half awake and half dreaming. As I developed the background of the painting, I thought that the mottled area behind the blue figure body looked like a wing, so I accentuated that aspect and instantly turned the figure into an angel.

The painting I made that day turned out to be a happy accident. It was full of surprise discoveries, and it unexpectedly became a piece of artwork that would have a lasting influence on all my other creations. One could say this blue angel was the first citizen of the Deviant Moon.

"Blue Angel", watercolor (1979, Age 12)

XV. The Devil

On a volcanic globe covered in sulfur and ash, the Devil dances in wicked delight; amused by the anarchy he has brought to the city. Once a glorious angel, he is now only a sad vision of beauty's decay. His useless wings have withered long ago, and his rotten skin barely covers the bones of his soulless body. A coward by nature, the Devil works his trickery from afar, manipulating minds in a sinister trance. Many have succumbed to his deceptive charm, believing his hollow promise of earthly gain. His negative influence ruins all inspiration and corrupts worthy thoughts with evil fantasies.

While the Devil wages a never-ending campaign to bind and oppress the souls of the people, he cannot enslave what is not given to him freely. All have the power within to resist, for his bindings are merely an illusion and are easily broken by choice. Although shunned by the universe and condemned to eternal exile, the Devil will always find a home in any heart offering refuge.

Upright meanings:

Destructive thinking patterns aspire to manipulate every aspect of your life. Unfortunately, you often blame your dismal situation on unseen forces that seem beyond your control. Understand that the Devil personifies your own diabolical ego, which seeks to restrict your mind through false limitations. Empowering thoughts and ideas find themselves bound to the psychological prison you have created within yourself. Know that you alone possess the power to break free of the mental chains that detain your spirit.

Under the hypnotic spell of the Devil, detrimental behaviors somehow seem alluring. Obsessive desires seek to dictate your actions, and you might find it difficult to resist physical temptation. Greed will try to rule your heart and force you to spend your days in an unwavering pursuit of material gain. Harmful addictions may consume you. The joy of life could be lost to the oppressive demands of your self-absorbed mindset.

Reversed meanings:

New ways of thinking will set your spirit free! The Devil in reverse suggests that the self-defeating thoughts that once limited your potential no longer have any power over your mind. Empowering solutions to your problems will reveal themselves as you come to realize that you alone control your destiny. Negativity will give way to a new and promising vision of what is possible in your life.

"The Devil" (1975, Age 8)

"The Witch in the Wall Comes Out!" (1975)

"The Angel with God" (1975)

"Demon with Burnt Skeleton" (1975)

Uncanny Inspiration

The Devil card in the Deviant Moon Tarot has no fancy props. It is entirely character driven. This illustration was influenced by one of my earliest memories. When I was about three years old, I got a tiny rubber devil out of a gumball machine. He was in the old fashioned style; long body, horns, pointy tail, and a little pitchfork. It was quite an intriguing little character. I remember studying its features and wondering about the mischievous grin. I used to sleep with the rubber devil under my pillow until one night it simply vanished. Although I never found it, the style of that small toy found its way into many of my first drawings.

My earliest surviving drawings are from a book I made just after discovering the tarot in 1975. The story is about a little girl who is afraid of the witch that lives in her wall. One night, the witch comes out and steals the little girl, taking her to down to the fires of Hell to be the slave of the Devil. In the end, she becomes an angel and winds up meeting God, who accidentally swallows her!

I made many storybooks like this when I was eight years old; most are long lost. Inspired by the imagery of tarot, I created one story after the other, and my artistic ability grew tremendously in a very short time. The more books I made for myself, the better I became at drawing. This result was never my intention. To me, expressing my imagination so others could see it was always my main goal. Art was an unexpected yet welcomed afterthought.

XVI. The Tower

The Tower stands ominously atop a dreary, gray globe, symbolic of the archaic traditions and beliefs that are often instituted upon one's mind. Without warning, the sky discharges an intense beam of light, striking the old structure with concentrated energy. The force of the blast penetrates the ancient brick walls and rocks the building down to its foundation.

Two wicked men fall victim to this devastating event. The first has leapt from the crumbling edifice, choosing to die on his own terms instead of allowing a divine force to consume him. On the ground lies the second sinner, who tries to protect himself from the impending avalanche of rubble in vain. Though they may try to resist their fate, the evil deeds of these doomed men will inevitably come to a tragic end. The powerful ray of light will quickly disintegrate the entire building, and all will collapse into ruin.

The black and white hands of these two cowardly men represent dualism. This concept can be interpreted as mind versus matter, physical versus spiritual, or good versus evil. Each area must have balance, so one side does not dominate the other. In this card, we see the destruction of the physical world by ethereal powers. The Tower itself expresses the rampant rise of man's materialistic ego while the lightning bolt is the spiritual force keeping everything in check.

Upright meanings:

The catastrophic destruction of the Tower forewarns of a severe or abrupt change. As painful as it may seem, you must realize that this upheaval will ultimately be in your best interest. Find comfort in knowing that a new and better existence will emerge from this traumatic incident.

Like a thunderbolt, disruptive events will jolt you out of your comfort zone! A sudden shift in your thinking pattern will cause you to reevaluate the age-old philosophies you cling to. Act swiftly and tear down the long-standing lies! Focus your mental energy into a directed beam of willpower and cleanse your mind of built up negativity. Obliterate your fears and rid yourself of old thoughts. Prepare to establish a new, enlightened way of thinking.

Reversed meanings:

When reversed, the Tower clearly shows that you are resistant to accepting an unsettling situation. Fear and uncertainty distract your mental focus, allowing your false beliefs to remain standing. Know that a turbulent change is unavoidable, and must be endured. You may also find yourself unable to break free from sad or disturbing events.

THE REAL TOWER

The Tower pictured in the Deviant Moon Tarot is an actual structure, which has fascinated my imagination for as long as I can remember. Constructed in 1930, this decrepit water tower stands abandoned and lonely on the grounds of Pilgrim State Asylum, isolated from the rest of the buildings. A large cemetery for unclaimed patients can be found nearby.

The tower looms ominously over the Long Island Expressway. As a child, I often wondered about it as we passed by in the family car, thinking of the odd princesses that might be trapped behind its gloomy brick walls.

Contractors have demolished many of the old asylum buildings to make way for condominiums. They currently plan to leave the water tower intact, however, so it can become the focal point of the new community.

The Water Tower at Pilgrim State
Psychiatric Hospital, N.Y., left

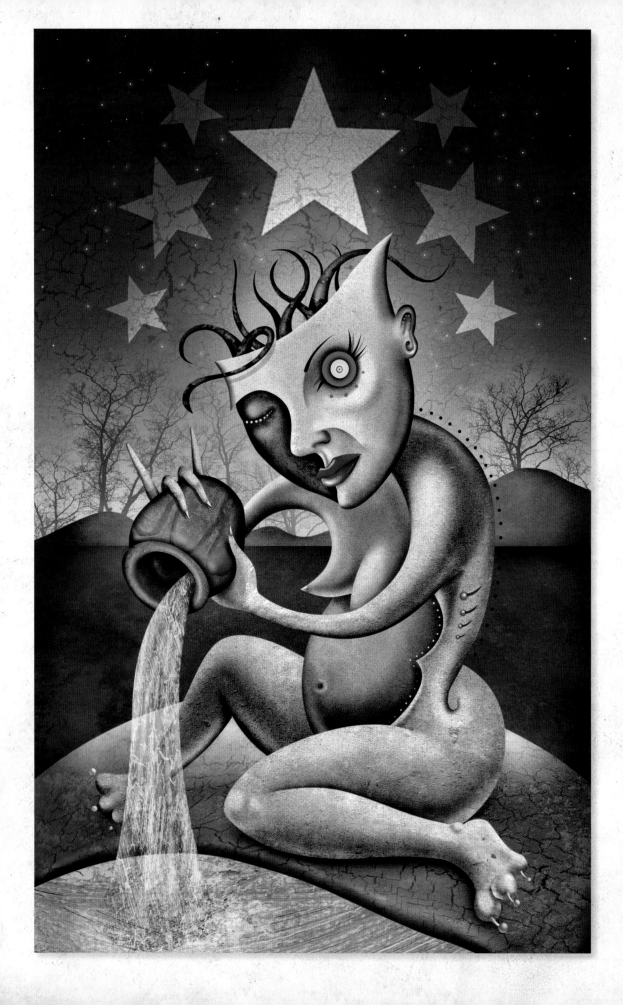

XVII. The Star

In a realm plagued by drought and starvation, a young maiden pours fresh water into a crystal clear pool. Day after day, she comes to this infertile spot to quench the thirst of the dry land. Though in need of fluid herself, she willingly gives up her meager supply to the parched earth, trusting it will nourish the hardened soil. In time, her selfless deed may give rise to succulent vegetation that will replenish this bleak landscape.

The maiden acts out of pure faith, with no guarantee that her work will be successful. Confidence in her ability allows her to envision a thriving future while others see only desolation. She does not dwell on the scarcity in her world, but keeps a fixed mind on the fruitful results she desires. When misfortune tries to dissuade the maiden's dreams, divine inspiration guides and encourages her ambitions. From above, seven gold stars shimmer optimistically in the sky, bringing hope and a bit of good luck to the forsaken wastelands below.

Upright meanings:

Let the glittering light of the Star lead you to a life of fulfillment! When this welcomed card appears in a reading, it serves as a bright sign of hope to a weary mind. Be assured that better days are yet to come. The haze of uncertainty clouding your thoughts will disperse, revealing an optimistic and inspired blessing from beyond. By thinking clearly, you will notice and appreciate the miracles that have always been around you, even at your most desperate times. Opportunities will open up, and you will finally surmount hard times. Though the prospects of a brilliant destiny may be exciting, you must be patient in your anticipation. Understand that a positive outcome will take time and will not come without sacrifice or hard work.

The Star also beckons you to cleanse your body, mind, and spirit. Bathe and rejuvenate your soul in its healing light. Nourish yourself, both physically and emotionally. Rid yourself of the impurities that lay your life to waste. Direct your thoughts and promise to maintain a positive outlook, regardless of what transpires around you.

Reversed meanings:

When you see the Star in reverse, it implies that you are unable to visualize a prosperous future. Efforts to improve unfavorable conditions seem hopeless. You may have lost your bearings in life or feel a lack of guidance from above. Inspiration that once flowed freely has dried up. Sadly, your skeptical and pessimistic attitude hinders your potential. Your disillusioned mind lingers on redundant thoughts that magnify all that is wrong in any given situation. Stress is the only thing growing in this emotionally barren environment.

Star of the Show

The maiden pictured on the Star card originated as a bongo player! She was a member of an eclectic jazz trio featured in a painting I created many years ago. Parts of this giant painting can be found hanging on the walls of the artist's studio in the Seven of Cups. I was never fond of the piece, but I always loved the essence of the little demon girl. The kneeling character filled the role in the star card perfectly. Rather than lose her in rejected artwork, I revised her appearance and gave her a permanent home in the Deviant Moon Tarot.

"Jazz Band", acrylic (1989), left

XVIII. The Moon

The bewildered King and Queen skip wildly through the night, intoxicated by the hypnotic power of a full moon. The moon above manipulates their thoughts like a puppeteer, sending silvery strings of lunar energy into their subconscious minds. Though entangled in a subliminal web, the royal pair experiences a newfound freedom. With reality distorted by illusion, they brush aside their rigid etiquette, allowing hidden personalities to emerge.

The King forsakes his majestic role, for tonight he plays the fool. No longer inhibited, he contorts his body in an expressive dance. Repressed creativity flows from his soul, manifesting into a poetic song, which he sings at the top of his lungs. Influenced through her emotions, the Queen lets go of her heartless and insensitive ways. For the moment, she is drunk with a passion for life, symbolized by the red rose she grips in her hand. Her dreaming eye loses itself in wild thoughts of love and romance. Twisting their legs together and howling with crazed laughter, the delirious couple runs amok down the streets of the city.

Reality is in the mind of the beholder! The deviant Moon tugs on mental strings tied to preexisting thoughts and emotions. It does not create behaviors, but only pulls them out from the shadows of our psyche. The Moon has not misled the King or Queen into their bizarre actions. It has only cast its alluring glow on the way they might perceive life.

Upright meanings:

The Moon characterizes the subliminal influence your subconscious mind has over you. It secretly commands your entire personality, while serving as a bridge between you and the unlimited ingenuity of the universe. Tune your thoughts to these intuitive brainwaves. Decipher what your mysterious dreams have to tell and allow the interpretation to guide you during the day. Let your imagination run free! Unlock the gates of your mind and release hidden desires and stifled emotions.

Under the spell of the moon, you might notice an increased sense of clairvoyance or other inexplicable psychic abilities. Repressed memories may also be trying to express themselves.

As you come to embrace your subconscious psyche, be aware that it could be deceptive at times. Memories, emotions and behaviors might become tangled in a knot of twisted trickery, leaving you unable to discern reality from fantasy. The Moon card might also warn of dark forces attempting to hijack your mind. Be wary of the psychological persuasion of those around you. Do not let them dictate your destiny with their mental games. Remember that you alone are ultimately in charge of your own thoughts.

Reversed meanings:

When it appears upside down, the Moon accentuates delusional thinking. You might feel as if you are losing control of your sanity as a long buried mental illness digs its way to the

surface. Confusion will strangle your mind with lies, choking all imagination and creativity. Sleep and other natural cycles may be interrupted without apparent cause. Unsettling nightmares will rule your dreams and haunt your waking hours. A reversed Moon is also an indicator of high-strung emotions and mood swings. You may become withdrawn in an effort to avoid reality, as unsociable or disorderly behaviors take hold of your personality.

ROYAL INFLUENCES

The design of the Moon card was inspired by visits to my grandparents' house at the age of four. They were both avid card players, and if you were a guest in their house, they compelled you to participate in a few hands. My grandparents' games were dead serious, and they usually banished children from the room when they played. I often snuck in anyhow and hid under the table so I could listen to their spirited conversations. One memorable night, I sat quietly on a bench watching their insane game. Behind me was a wide-open window, through which I could see a bright, full moon floating in the night sky. I was convinced that this glowing orb was alive and that his happy, round face was smiling right at me.

As I sat there staring in wonder at the lunar miracle before me, my grandmother gave me a few old cards to keep me amused while they played. My attention turned to the intriguing royal characters I held in my young hands. As my eyes absorbed the artwork, I imagined the king and queen running through the neighborhood outside the window, laughing under the light of the magnificent moon. That vision embedded itself in my mind and profoundly influenced my peculiar imagination. It is incredible how a tiny event in one's life can significantly shape the course of the future. From that night on, I would be forever entranced by the mesmeric allure of the moon. My newfound love for art of playing cards led me to discover the tarot only a few years later.

The Deviant Moon has two different faces because I found a better texture source midway through the deck's creation and never replaced the earlier versions. Each face is a photo manipulation made from 18th century tombstone carvings.

"The Moon", colored pencil (1980, Age 13)
(Black background digitally added for clarity.)

XIX. The Sun

The omniscient sun rises in the morning sky, bringing with it the miracle of a new day. Its brilliant light dissolves the darkness of the night and awakens sleepy minds from bad dreams. As the clouds of confusion melt away, the rain that once drenched the land in sorrow change into blazing drops of vibrant energy.

The sun shines over the city and bestows joyful blessings on a pair of youthful lads. The boys have come together in separate physical forms, yet their spiritual consciousness unites them. Meeting here for the first time, they find themselves instantly attracted to each other through their similarities. Shared traits lead to a strong rapport, which will soon develop into a lasting, harmonious relationship. Undivided by walls, the twins stand arm in arm, creating a bridge of friendship. With souls joined and bodies invigorated by the sun's rays, they embark on the day's journey together.

Upright meanings:

Glorious days are ahead! When the Sun comes up in a reading, it proclaims an end to dark times and the beginning of a new era of fulfillment. This life-giving entity will usher in a golden season of intense happiness and pure joy. A revitalized enthusiasm for life will come over you, which will immeasurably enhance every aspect of your existence. Allow this vibrant passion to emanate from your personality and influence everyone you meet. Know that you can achieve greatness through the cooperation of like-minded people who share your ascending aspirations.

It is time to ignite your genius and reveal your mental brilliance. An enlightened state of consciousness is ready to dawn upon you. New ideas will burst forth from your energized mind, breaking through the haze of ignorance and self-doubt. By thinking clearly, you will light your world with shining success.

Along with the renewal of your mental energy, the Sun represents robust vitality, rejuvenation, and physical well-being. By nurturing and strengthening your body, you will experience glowing good health. Healing will take its natural course, and save you from illness. Your stamina will dramatically increase, giving you the power to turn your nighttime dreams into the reality of your day.

Reversed meanings:

When in reverse, the Sun appears to be setting on your ambitions. Thoughts are clouded, energy is low, and confidence is sinking. Happiness seems elusive. You may feel unfulfilled regardless of the blessings that shine upon you. This inability to see the bright side of unpleasant situations blocks your potential for greatness. Realize that the enlightenment you seek is near, but you must concentrate your efforts to find it.

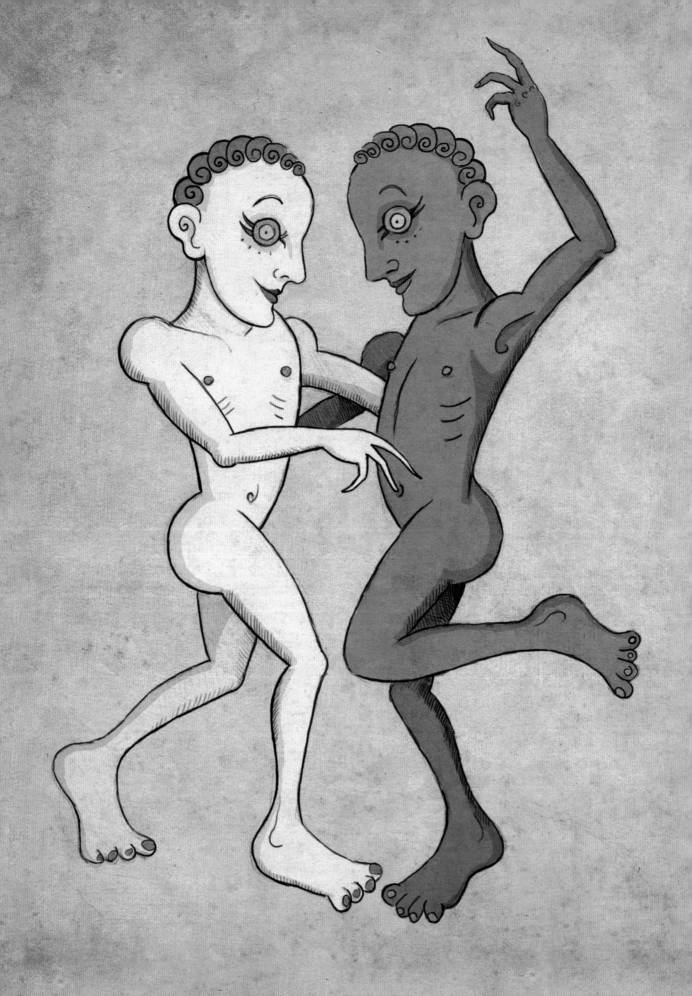

As the sun goes down, friendships may be strained or ended. There will be difficulty cooperating with others as negative personalities come out to play. Know that you must first examine yourself to find a solution to your unstable relationships.

THE SISTER DECK

As I was completing the remaining cards of the deck, I began to realize that the nighttime world I had been creating for over 30 years was coming to an end. I was happy to see my life's imagination come to fruition, yet sad to think I would be forever done with the characters and their stories. Every card in the Deviant Moon Tarot had a little part of my soul in it, along with a piece of every strange idea I ever had. I thought I would be saying goodbye to this midnight realm and expected to move on to other projects.

While working on the very last card (Six of Pentacles), a bright vision suddenly struck me. The citizens of the Deviant Moon had awakened from their dream, and they had a great deal more to say. New characters, costumes, and settings where revealed to me in a flash of insight. The idea for a deck ruled by the Sun overwhelmed my imagination.

This sequel will be the sister to the Deviant Moon Tarot. Like a true sibling, she will have many family characteristics, as well as her own distinct personality and temperament. In no way will she be her brother's clone, for her beauty is all her own. Using wisdom and a little bit of charm, she will empower conscious thoughts and open minds to bright possibilities.

In this early design for the boys, a white and a black child dance together in harmony. I felt that the duality they expressed fit the swordsman in the Two of Swords much better, so in the end, I changed the pair into identical twins.

"Carefree Lads" (2005)

XX. Judgment

In a flash of brilliant light, a dark cloud reveals the Angel of Judgment over the morning sky. Crafted out of tombstones, his wings are a reassuring metaphor showing that death frees the spirit so it can fly off to a higher plane of existence. Behind the Angel's golden crown, we see the arc of a distant rainbow, giving all a glimpse into the blissful world beyond the grave. With a mighty blast from his trumpet, he awakens the dead from their dreamless sleep. Three corpses rise out of a decrepit tomb, brought back to life by the mysterious sound of an ethereal calling. The first corpse guards her infant from this divine apparition. In life, she had become fearful of the spirit realm and anything she was unable to see with her own eyes. In death, she continues to cling to her misgivings, unconvinced by the glorious vision she now beholds.

The second corpse smacks his forehead in profound realization; his mind a witness to the miracle before him. Throughout life, he had denied the existence of a spiritual plane, explaining it away with logic and empirical evidence. This morning, the universe has revealed its truths before him, yet he turns his head the other way. He prefers to slump back into his hole rather than see his mistaken beliefs disproved.

The third cadaver spent his days on earth committing crimes against his fellow citizens. He was heartless and cruel; never caring for anything but his own gain. Ironically, he begs the angelic entity for the compassion he never practiced himself. His attempts are in vain, however, for he cannot bargain his way into redemption.

Time has run out for this trio of egotistical creatures. Their souls have been dead long before the demise of their physical bodies. Each has squandered their precious days on earth, absorbed in themselves and oblivious to the true purpose of life. The angel offers forgiveness to them regardless of their mortal faults and misdeeds. Yet even on this day of mercy, they are reluctant to forsake their depraved ways and reconnect to their spiritual origins.

Upright meanings:

Listen to the call of your divine spirit. The Judgment card beckons us to awaken from our ego-driven mindset and become the loving, spiritual energy we truly are. By shedding old thoughts and beliefs that keep us entombed, we will usher in a new era of fulfillment to our earthly existence. Although a new beginning is at hand, you must account for past offenses. Don't attempt to bury these transgressions, for they will ultimately be exposed in the end. Make a conscious decision to change your ways. Be honest with yourself. Clear your mind and learn from your mistakes. Now is the time to transform your lifeless days into the inspired experiences they were destined to be!

Watercolor (1985)   *"Mother and Child Revived"*

Reversed meanings:

In a reversed position, the Judgment card implies that you are punishing yourself for past mistakes and worrying over possible consequences. Self-condemnation will not allow you to let go of your guilt. Sadly, you are ignoring the call to a higher purpose. Fearful thoughts concerning your mortality leave you unable to transcend the limits set by your ego.

Years ago, I rendered my illustrations in either colored pencil or rough, watercolor sketches. The work was extremely time consuming and ultimately impractical for publication. I often lost focus, jumping from one project to the next. Overstuffed portfolios became artistic mausoleums, housing hundreds of unfinished drawings. Abandoned ideas and forgotten characters were rotting away on the old paper, begging to be resurrected.

I began experimenting with computer graphics because I was curious to see how my neglected drawings might appear in a new digital medium. The first drawing I brought back to life was of a young mother holding her infant. The shapes were extremely basic, and I simply traced over the old piece. I had no idea how to operate the art programs, but I knew what I wanted to achieve, and learned by hitting every button until I got the results I desired. I loved that I was able to apply textures, manipulate photographs, or change any aspect of the piece instantly. Speed was another benefit of this newfound tool. A pencil drawing took a few weeks to create, yet the digital version took me only a day. Inspired by the possibilities, I began to revive my life-long tarot ideas. The little infant found on the Judgment card pays tribute to my first digital work and symbolizes the reawakening of my artistic and creative spirit.

Concept sketches (2004)

XXI. The World

A triumphant young woman returns to the city after completing a successful journey around the world. She has acquired extraordinary skills along the way, and the experience has transformed her into a beautiful mermaid. Adorned with the precious artifacts earned on her travels, she celebrates the rewards of her hard work and diligent efforts. As she dances in excitement, the mermaid joyfully twirls two candles burning at both ends around in her hands. This signifies her willingness to do without rest in the pursuit of her dreams. The jeweled crab set on her collar represents her commitment and tenacity. Her majestic crown of pearls and shells symbolizes the vital role her mind has played in achieving her ambitions.

The mermaid gratefully thanks the universe for guiding her through her odyssey over land and sea. She points a finger to the heavens, indicating her alignment with divine energy. This relationship has enabled her to overcome secular obstacles by strengthening her spirit during adversity. Today, she arrives home refined by the hardships she has endured. The sun shining in the background embodies her newly-awakened consciousness. It rises over the city and serenely watches a sailing vessel as it navigates the waters of a subconscious ocean. Like the ship, the mermaid has come back to her place of origin, ready to deliver her worldly insights to all citizens.

The fierce animals surrounding the mermaid symbolize various aspects of her enlightened voyage. By learning to master her emotions, she has developed the power to tame the wild beasts of doubt and fear; both now sit passively below her. Above, two fish leap out of the water and into the air, leaving behind the fluid comfort of their dream state. They have taught the mermaid how to bring her own submerged thoughts and desires into reality by breaking through the surface of her perceived limitations.

The large Ouroboros encircling the mermaid separates time and events. Outside of the circle, we see the mermaid's dismal past covered in darkness and lined with barren trees,

while a magnificent vision of the present moment occupies the inside. The snake-like Ouroboros devours its own tail, showing that the conclusion of one cycle merely marks the start of another. With her global trek now behind her, the mermaid is ready to begin an inspired future filled with endless possibilities.

Upright meanings:

Begin your cycle of success today. The World card illustrates the successful culmination of hard work and persistent effort. It depicts a moment of celebration and the fulfillment of ambitions. Understand, however, that your noble dreams will only be realized after you have actively pursued them. Success will not come to you by chance, nor will the heavens freely bestow it upon you as a divine gift. The results you desire will arrive in response to the amount of energy you are willing to put forth. Do not sit idly by as the world moves around you! Transcend the illusionary thoughts that hold you back and take the first step towards attaining your destiny right now.

Know that the path to success will never be easy. You must be willing to take risks and endure great sacrifices along the way. Have faith and trust in your undiscovered abilities. Visualize your destination and then consciously guide your mind in the right direction every day. Collect your small daily achievements as you make your way through life and build them into a tremendous victory in the end.

Reversed meanings:

Your life is drifting off course! When reversed, the World becomes a card mired in frustration. Fear and doubt have taken control of your uncertain mind, causing you to lose sight of your ambitions. Goals seem distant and impossible to achieve. This is because you often leave projects incomplete, allowing promising endeavors to fail. Perhaps you get easily discouraged by minor setbacks, and are unable to see the opportunities hidden in adversity. Understand that this limited way of thinking keeps you from expanding past your short-sighted mental horizons.

As I completed the World card, I thought about my tarot journey over the last three decades. I had just spent the last two years pulling my childhood ideas together, recreating and finally finishing the Major Arcana. At that time, I had no vision for the Minors, and never intended to work on them at all. I honestly thought this tarot creation was at its end, but as the World tells us; the end of one endeavor only marks the beginning of another.

Pre-Mermaid sketch (2005), left

"Wild Beasts" (2005)

A few nights after completing the Major Arcana, I had a vivid dream featuring medieval moon-faced characters running around with swords. The next day, I tried to capture my visions in earnest. I quickly created drawings for the King, Queen, and Knight of Swords. When I finished, I simply closed my sketchbook and put it back on the shelf. I still had no intention of continuing the deck, but instead wished to explore a totally new and different project. That very night, I had another intense dream where I specifically saw several cards fully finished and alive. I woke up very early that morning and sketched the entire suit of Swords in one frantic day. I knew then that the deck was demanding to be completed.

Until this point, few people had ever seen any of the cards as I tended to keep my artwork hidden. I had created them for myself, and never planned to have them published. Something inside, however, told me the deck 'wanted' to be shown now. I sent a few samples to U.S. Games Systems, Inc. expecting the deck to be rejected. To my astonishment, I received a contract for its publication! This truly made me feel like the mermaid in the World card! All of my efforts had paid off, and now a new door of opportunity was opening up for me. Inspired, I eagerly set off to work on the Minor Arcana. Working more diligently than ever, I finished the next 56 cards within a year.

Minor Arcana

The four realms of the Minor Arcana can be easily identified by their border colors in the original deck. While the various border colors found in the Major Arcana were chosen simply for aesthetic reasons, the colors in the Minors also convey the overall characteristics of each suit.

Swords—Red:	Conflict. Heartfelt strife. Anxiety. Danger.
Wands—Green:	Nature. New beginnings. Creativity. Fertility. Growth.
Cups—Blue:	Water. Subconscious thought. Peace and tranquility.
Pentacles—Black:	Materialism. Industrious work. Spiritual void.

Unlike most of the Major Arcana, I did not conceive the Minor cards in my childhood. I created them as an adult by putting myself into a childlike state of mind. I needed to tap into my young, unhindered imagination by allowing my past to take control of my present. I spent a few weeks revisiting old schoolyards, lost sketchbooks, and forgotten family photographs in order to bring my thoughts back to the times when I was most prolific. When I was ready to begin sketching, I even configured my studio to resemble my workspace of 30 years ago and played the same sappy 70s Top 40 songs I listened to back then. This technique worked amazingly well to awaken my intuitive mind and spirit in ways I never dreamed were possible. One after the other, the images began to appear on the sketch paper with little effort. It honestly felt as if they were manifesting themselves into existence, and I was merely a spectator to their inspired creation.

A suitable name for my tarot deck had long eluded me. I spent years searching for the perfect title, but none seemed to fit. Not long after completing the Majors, something whispered the name Deviant Moon into my imagination. Hearing those words in my mind was like a mysterious friend giving me the secret answer to an unsolvable puzzle! The title expressed the dark, peculiar mood of the deck and in turn, affected the creation of the Minor Arcana. The moon would now play a more prominent role in the cards that followed. It not only added personified mischief to the night, but influenced the lunar aspects of the citizens as well.

Suit of Swords

Though they possess great power and wealth, the Family of Swords trouble themselves with turmoil and conflict. Misguided by their egos, they falsely believe that life has been cruel to them, denying the notion that their mental wounds may, in fact, be self-inflicted. The citizens of this kingdom cannot blame the outside world for their pain and misery. To find peace, they must take responsibility for their own emotional well-being and discover empowering solutions within themselves to overcome life's adversities.

King of Swords

The King of Swords governs his people and his own emotions with disciplined control. He lives by the letter of law and expects his kingdom to do the same. The broad sword held in his hand represents his straightforward ability to take decisive action and cut to the heart of any situation. The King is not influenced by the ambiguity of feelings. Instead, he relies on cold facts when making important rulings. Though his impersonal approach to life gives order to his ego, it often leads to a lack of empathy towards others.

The King wears the emblem of the moon across his chest while the true moon hangs in the distant sky. This symbolic relationship shows that he is guided by the implied reality of the physical world and does not consult his subconscious for insight. By pushing his emotions far out of range, he can master his own his mental state without interference.

A henchman from the royal army crouches by the king's side clinging tight to a small globe. He challenges all with his hypnotic stare, using intimidation to enforce the King's overbearing authority throughout the land.

Upright meanings:

Dominate your problems. The King of Swords personifies unwavering determination and willpower. Like him, you need to take firm command of the situation at hand. Important choices must be made that will require clear and objective analysis. Be sure to investigate your options and develop a sound strategy to solve your dilemmas. Think logically and set your emotions aside. Although such calculated decisions may seem callous, know that they are ultimately in the best interest of all involved. Remain steadfast and hold true to your values!

Reversed meanings:

When reversed, the King of Swords presents himself as a strict and unyielding personality. This could come in the form of a controlling authority figure in your life, or it might

*King of Swords,
sketch (2006)*

manifest in your own tyrannical actions. Whatever the case, someone may be ignoring extenuating circumstances in a ruthless enforcement of rules. Know that harsh verdicts and cruel decisions may soon be rendered.

After completing the initial sketches for the Minor Arcana, I went out to find new and unique textures to apply into the fashions of the citizens. My hunt led me to explore Green-Wood cemetery in Brooklyn. There, I spent several days taking photographs of various tombstones and mausoleums. I wound up with over 5,000 photos to work with by the time I returned home.

I first created the textured outfit for the King of Swords, which inspired the wardrobe style for the rest of the royal family. The royals then set a precedent for the color palette used throughout the suit.

To create the King's lower body, I used a tombstone that happened to have the word 'sister' on it. Perhaps it was merely a coincidence, but I received a cell phone call from my own sister only a few minutes after I took this shot.

Gravestones were not the only texture used in the making of this card. I created the little minion holding the globe from a photo of a rusted lock.

Queen of Swords

H oping to escape the turmoil, which pervades her life, the Queen of Swords seeks refuge in a secluded forest. In her endeavor to find peace and comfort, however, she sadly discovers that her troubles follow along too. The deviant moon mutters over her shoulder reminding the weeping Queen of her anxiety and distress. The Queen chooses not to face her subconscious tormentor, but instead has become a martyr to her own self-pity.

The Queen's powerful position is no consolation for the loneliness felt within her heart. She views life with teary eyes and sees a distorted world through the mesh of her mourning veil. Her depressing thoughts transform the beauty of the surrounding trees into the iron bars of an emotional prison.

The Queen's conflicted soul causes her to grind two swords together. The painful friction produces blood at the end of one blade, which drips and splatters onto the path before her. With agony ruling her mind, she will surely follow the bloody stains into a future filled with misery.

Upright meanings:

When the despondent Queen of Swords wanders into your reading, she is merely looking for another place to hide from the sorrow that stalks her. Like her, your thoughts and emotions may be trapped in an endless pattern of negativity. Your subconscious seems haunted by worry, guilt and regret. Though your pain may be real, understand that you suffer by choice. Let go of your anguish. The Queen burdens herself with two swords, yet she can easily drop them to the ground at any time. You can do the same too! Decide at once to rid yourself of the angst that shreds your heart to pieces. Realize that you can never run away from yourself. In order to find the tranquility you desire, you must courageously confront the persecutor dwelling inside of your own mind.

The Queen of Swords may also represent someone who has experienced the loss of a loved one. This individual is unable to free herself from overwhelming grief and sadness. She is emotionally fragile and sheds infinite tears. She feels disconnected from life, and often spends her days searching the dreary corners of her mind for the person she misses the most.

Reversed meanings:

When reversed, the Queen signifies someone who holds on to grief in a subconscious attempt to gain sympathy from others. This person exaggerates her misfortunes for dramatic effect and then thrives on the attention. Pain has become part of her identity. She plays the victim well, using life's burdens as props in a self-created tragedy.

Queen of Swords, sketch (2006)

In the final image, drops of red nail polish were used to achieve the desired blood effect on the ground.

Knight of Swords

Unwilling to stay confined to his mundane post, the Knight of Swords mounts his savage steed and prepares to embark on a self-absorbed mission. Impulsive by nature, he gives no thought to the consequence of leaving the city unprotected. His allegiance is to himself, and his ego knows no boundary. Though the Knight seeks to be free of his limitations, his spirit will always be encased in the armor he wears. Forged by vanity, it glistens with conceited pride. In the Knight's mind, the world belongs to him, and it is his divine right to take it by whatever means necessary. Those who challenge his narcissistic aspirations will find themselves penetrated by his sharp sword and keen intellect.

The city gate is open wide, revealing a barren landscape in the distance. Although there are no urgent matters to attend to outside the castle walls, the arrogant Knight will surely create an emergency where none exists. Whether he builds a new kingdom far away or starts a fresh conflict in a foreign land remains to be seen.

The energetic Knight needs to be in constant motion. He will not wait around for life to come to him. He envisions possibilities beyond his present situation, and knows that now is the time to act upon his desires. Without hesitation, he valiantly grabs the reins of fear and begins the charge into the unknown, fully convinced that his brave actions can only lead to a heroic victory.

Upright meanings:

Seize the initiative! The Knight of Swords symbolizes the daring confidence you will need in order for your dreams to succeed. Be quick and courageously chase after your destiny. An enormous opportunity lies before you; however, you must leave your comfort zone and aggressively pursue it. Proceed with absolute certainty in your abilities, and do not falter. Be assertive and do what needs to be done, regardless of what others think or whom it may offend. Understand that your ambitions will only be realized by taking bold action in spite of your fear.

On the other hand, this card might indicate tactless behaviors. Self-serving motives override your true purpose in life. You might be forcing your opinions on others, and not taking their feelings into account. You may also be making a rash decision that can only result in trouble.

Reversed meanings:

When the Knight of Swords shows up in reverse, it implies that you are hesitant to seek out opportunity. You may be reluctant to venture away from familiar surroundings, or afraid to take risks. Fear keeps you stuck in unfavorable conditions, and as a result you are slow to respond to the calls of destiny.

Swords

7/12/06

As a child, I wanted a suit of armor to stand in the foyer of my future home. In fact, I imagined having one in each room, believing they would protect me from the ghosts that so often wandered around my mind. As an adult, I no longer wish to own such metallic monstrosities. Today, I would much rather have the ghosts!

The metallic textures for the Knight of Swords came from a dusty suit of armor I found standing in an antique shop.

Noble knights (Age 8?)

Knight of Swords, sketch (2006), left

Page of Swords

The Page of Swords begins his quest for personal insight after rejecting the beliefs imposed by his neurotic family. Though still in his youth, he has wisely decided that he alone must direct the course of his own life, regardless of any dysfunctional upbringing. His convictions lead him to separate from his brood and seek integrity amongst the citizens of the kingdom. As he roams the city, the Page comes to realize that the outside world is no different from the one he just left. Much like his family, the miserable people here do little to improve their own dismal existence.

As the young Page travels along, the night attempts to seduce him with her secrets. However, she foolishly underestimates the boy's keen determination to find virtue. Keeping his sword upright, the Page cuts through her trickery and continues his journey towards enlightenment. The perceptive light from his eye penetrates the darkness of the shadowy streets, exposing falsehoods and uncovering hidden pathways. By focusing the beam on solutions, the Page intuitively guides himself out of an emotionally impoverished situation and into the fulfilling life he so richly deserves.

Upright meanings:

The insightful Page of Swords demonstrates that you need not accept the depressing conditions that surround you. Follow the self-empowered path he blazes and let his bold actions serve as an example. Like him, you must open your mind in order to recognize unfamiliar possibilities. Always look for the good in every situation and use it to your advantage. Remember to take full responsibility for everything that happens to you. Regardless of your circumstances, you must remain true to yourself. Never let anyone discourage your ambitions. Trust that your talents and abilities will see you through even when there seems to be no hope in sight.

Reversed meanings:

Be forewarned! You may be overwhelmed by deception as unforeseen forces conspire to hinder your plans. Enter new situations with suspicion. Lies will obscure your path, leaving you confused over whom or what to trust. Friends who claim to have your best interest at heart secretly plot your downfall.

*Page of Swords,
sketch (2006)*

The Page's eyepiece came from a pair of antique binoculars I have owned since childhood. When I was a boy, I often studied the moon through these magical lenses believing the dark craters I saw up close were expansive lunar oceans. As an adult, I still let my imagination run wild thinking of the cities I just might find if I look long and hard at the glowing surface.

Antique binoculars

Ten of Swords

Ten swords penetrate a wooden box, piercing the miserable yellow man trapped inside. Although sharp blades stab his flesh, the poor wretch does not bleed from his wounds. His injuries are purely psychological. While the swords pin his thoughts to misfortune, the dreary box squeezes the resolve out of his soul and crushes all inspiration. His limited beliefs have created the very walls that surround him, and he cannot foresee life outside of his claustrophobic existence.

Even in the face of imminent death, the yellow man does not struggle or attempt an escape. He accepts his suffering as unavoidable and has willingly surrendered to his fate. Before long, the box will sadly become his coffin. Wracked with unbearable pain, the dying man curls up and withers in agony. He takes one final breath before drifting out of consciousness and into eternal sleep where he will ultimately find the peaceful sanctuary he longs for at last.

Upright meanings:

External forces are violently assaulting the serenity of your psyche. You may find yourself unable to withstand the negative influences of your environment as destructive thoughts thrust themselves upon your mind. Although you have no power over these outside invaders, you must remember that you have absolute authority over your internal realm. Refuse to be victimized by your circumstances! Know that you are emotionally strong enough to repel the onslaught of a sadistic world. Stretch your possibilities and expand your options. Break out of the mental confines that keep you helplessly entombed in a grim predicament.

The Ten of Swords also forewarns of utter despair and agonizing defeat. Be prepared for what might appear to be inescapable suffering. The prolonged ordeal you might undergo could ultimately reach the point of torture. Pain may come at you from every angle as you find yourself overwhelmed by multiple problems. Miserable events could culminate in a tragic ending.

Reversed meanings:

When reversed, the Ten of Swords predicts a slight easing of your pain and torment. You now have the chance to get the upper hand over your hardships. The worst is over; however, it will still be a tremendous struggle to reach equilibrium in your life. In this position, the card could also foretell of a brief period of relief during catastrophic times. Use this occasion to gather your strength as you brace for another wave of agony.

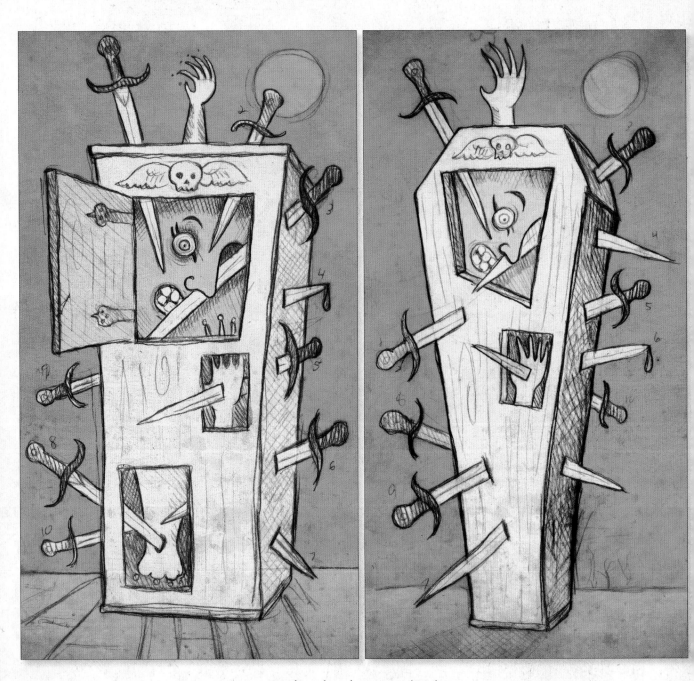

Ten of Swords, early variations (2006)

Boxed for Death

One of the memories I have always had was that of being trapped inside of an old chest. This vision comes as a climactic finale to what I consider my most dramatic past life experience. Images and emotions from these strange times are responsible for the person I am today, and they continue to influence the core of my imagination. Although these memories are clear and powerful, they have always been fragmented. Putting them together the best I can, I offer you the following uncanny events.

I was among a small group of men assigned to track the movement of a band of renegade soldiers across the countryside. The leader of these traitors was a murderous character dressed as a harlequin. We discovered our enemies' camp one night and thought we had the rebels cornered. Peering through the planks of a large wooden stockade, I saw the elongated figure of the harlequin dancing around a roaring fire. He entertained his troops with a melancholic song as they roasted meat over the open flames. (To this day, the sweet aroma of seasoned meat evokes strange memories associated with this fateful evening.)

Without warning, the vile harlequin abruptly stopped his wicked romp and silently pointed his bony finger in our direction. Surprised by this show of clairvoyance, my men and I scattered into the darkness, hoping to escape. With torches blazing, our adversaries set out after us. They chased us through the forest and ruthlessly hunted us down. One by one, I heard the horrific screams of my comrades in the distance as they were caught and killed by the harlequin's henchmen.

"The Maniacal Harlequin" (Age 11)

I somehow managed to outlast the terror of the night. As the morning sun crept over the hills, I came across a small town. Knowing the assassins were still close behind, I searched for a place of refuge. I ran into what I believed to be a vacant tavern and made my way up to the top floor. I quickly found a large chest and hid myself inside, daring not to breathe. I thought I had lost my predators until I heard them crash into the building and rush upstairs. The heavy sound of footsteps pounded on the wooden floorboards and then stopped outside of the chest where I lay curled up. My mind panicked, wondering how they could have known where I was.

I expected the killers to thrust the lid open, leaving me exposed and vulnerable. Instead, I heard the clanking of metal outside the box and some loud banging. Then they lifted the chest and carried me downstairs. I tried to push the lid open with all my strength, but it was useless. With me still crammed inside, the henchmen threw the chest into a lake. The last memory I have is of cold water streaming through the cracks of the wood as I slowly sunk to my death.

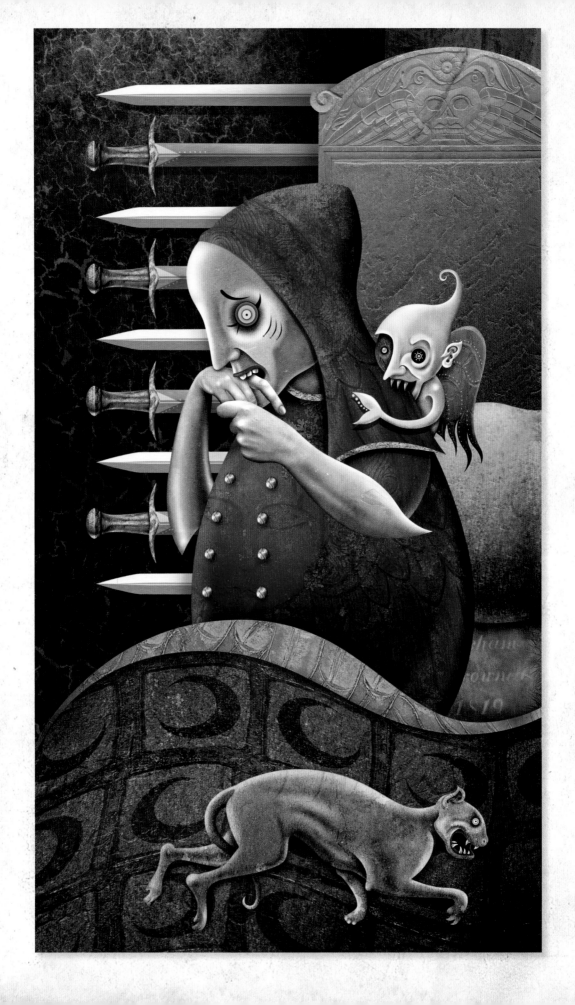

Nine of Swords

A nervous old woman quivers in the darkness, awakened by a dreadful nightmare. Unable to return to a peaceful sleep, she sits up in her bed, anxiously pulling her fingers and gnawing on her hand. The ghastly apparition of nine swords lingers in her mind as she tries in vain to distinguish reality from delusion. The mere thought of the blades intensifies her suffering and brings her to the edge of emotional collapse.

Frightful sensations crawl like insects over the woman's pale skin, infesting her head with worry. Her frenzied imagination exaggerates her phobias and horrifically brings them to life. Anxiety takes the shape of a mischievous white imp, who sneaks up from behind and stabs its sharp fangs into the woman's shoulder. Injected venom races through her veins, causing her heart to palpitate with panic. As the nasty imp nibbles the woman's flesh, it extends its toothed claw towards her vulnerable neck, knowing that a little snip to her throat will surely enhance the pain. Paralyzing fear expresses itself in the form of a mummified feline corpse, which lies like an immovable weight on top of her blanket. The cat's atrophied muscles signify that the old woman's overwhelming concerns cripple her spirit.

The warmth of the old woman's bed dissipates into the night, leaving only a tomblike chill under the covers. As morbid thoughts of death continue to twist around her senses, they change the way she perceives her surroundings. Her blanket no longer provides comfort, but now seems like dirt over a restless grave, while the ornate woodwork on the headboard appears in her mind as the ominous stone carvings of tombstone. The morning sun will soon rise, but it will fail to break the spell of her warped visions. Tonight, the seeds of despair have been firmly planted in her brain, and she will carry her nocturnal terror into the new day ahead.

Upright meanings:

In the gloom of the night, every shadow is suspect. When the foreboding Nine of Swords materializes in your reading, it is a dramatic sign that you are overly focused on your fears and anxieties. You may find yourself incapable of sleep, as your worried thoughts loop in an endless cycle of distress. Horrible notions twist your mind and heighten the suffering of your weary soul. Paranoia immobilizes your potential. Guilt and regret eat away at you without mercy, and you imagine the worst possible outcomes for the future. Irrational fixations over sickness and death relentlessly haunt you. These negative emotions could spiral out of control, leaving you susceptible to prolonged bouts of depression. You could also be experiencing excessive concerns over loved ones, or a preoccupation with things that you have no control over.

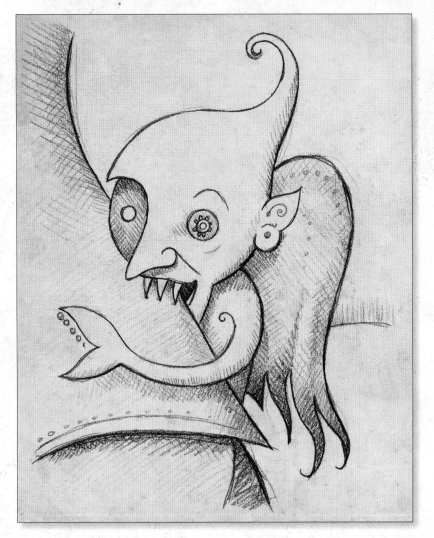

Reversed meanings:

When reversed, the Nine of Swords reveals a possible break in your negative thinking patterns. Optimistic and bright energies are trying to surface, but you must be willing to embrace them. Now is the time to stop obsessing over your fears. Decide not to waste another precious second of your life in suffering. Focus on your blessings instead of your worries. Admit to yourself that your concerns are overly dramatized and exaggerated. Remember to consciously direct your mind, or it will subconsciously direct you.

Fluffy

When I was in high school, my art teacher had us draw all kinds of odd objects to practice our skills. The oddest, but greatest of them all was affectionately known as Fluffy. Fluffy was a mummified cat gifted to him by a student many years before I came to his class. Fluffy's skin was like dried, brown cardboard and her tail like a wire. She wore a hideous grimace, and her dehydrated eyes were sunk deep into her skull. It was a real treat when the teacher brought her out to be sketched. Although Fluffy's appearance initially horrified the girls in the class, they soon got used to her and even pet her from time to time. I made many drawings of Fluffy during those years, yet all that exists today is a very small thumbnail sketch I did of her on the back of another artwork.

Over 20 years after I had last seen Fluffy, I woke up one night to find her apparition at the foot of my bed! The vision only lasted for a few seconds before she transformed into the folds of my blanket. Whether her appearance was a ghost or just a sleep-induced apparition, I will never know. Regardless, I loved the experience of seeing her after all that time. One thing I was sure of was that Fluffy wanted a part in the Deviant Moon deck, and I was more than happy to let her in. Using my old thumbnail sketch as a reference, I incorporated her into the Nine of Swords card. The mummified cat lying on the bed pays homage to her gruesome carcass, as well as to her strange nocturnal manifestation.

"Anxiety", sketch (2006), top

Thumbnail sketch of Fluffy (1984), bottom

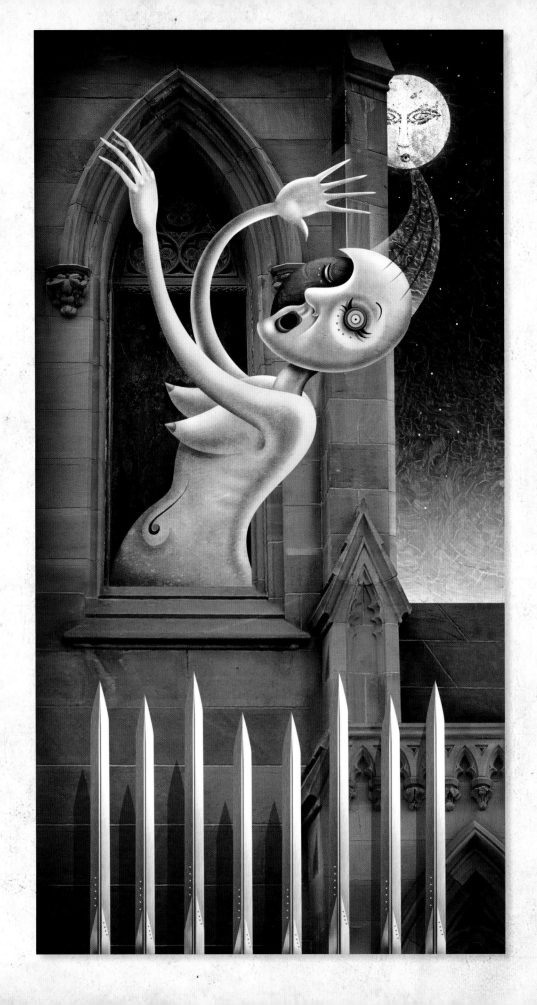

Eight of Swords

The hypnotic calls of the deviant moon lure a young woman out of her slumber. Lunar whispers reverberate inside her head and forcefully bind themselves to her thoughts. Half awake, the woman finds herself ripped from the safety of her cloistered tower and pulled against her will through an open window. She waves her arms with wild confusion as her drowsy mind ebbs into the night. Although the young woman struggles to regain control over her senses, she is powerless to break free from the grip of this mysterious nocturnal trance. Silence chokes her screams, and a mute plea for help goes unheard in the darkness. The wall inside her room glows red with pain, representing the trauma caused by this subconscious abduction.

Below the window, eight glimmering swords stand erect, poised to penetrate the woman's milky white body. The blades symbolize the imminent danger awaiting those who allow themselves to be manipulated by outside energies. If the woman fails to separate from these malicious subliminal connections, she will surely be impaled by a sharp reality.

In time, the young woman could be rescued from her ordeal, provided she lasts long enough for her liberator to arrive. Light rises in the distant sky; a reassuring sign that daybreak is near. Soon, the brilliant sun will chase away the shadows of sleep, and the moon's strange influence over the woman's dreams will come to an end.

Upright meanings:

Your thoughts do not seem to be your own. External forces drag your mind in an undesirable direction. You may find it impossible to concentrate as distractions dominate your life. Ideas go astray, and thoughts flow into oblivion. Perverse and abnormal urges may soon overtake your sound judgment. You could be suffering from an uncontrollable obsession, which will likely drain your energy and squander your potential for greatness. Additionally, you might be victimized by someone who persuasively exerts his will upon you.

This card might also forewarn of an unwelcomed change that will disrupt your emotional well-being. Such disturbances could be fear over an uncertain future, or being torn from a secure environment and exposed to the world before you are ready.

Reversed meanings:

When dealt in reverse, the Eight of Swords reveals that you will ultimately break free of your mental enslavement. Confidence in your abilities will emerge and empower you! No longer will you blindly follow the whims of others, or be controlled by deviant notions. Compulsive ideas will subside, and you will overcome any harmful habits or addictions. Your concentration will improve immensely, and you will be less distracted by outside demands. As you regain control of your mind, your focused thoughts will lead your life in the direction of your own choosing.

My first idea for the Eight of Swords pictured a woman running up a twisted flight of stairs while the deviant moon siphoned the thoughts from her mind. As I was sketching, it became apparent that there would be no meaningful way to position eight swords into this composition without them looking like an afterthought. This card taught me early on that the swords, wands, cups and pentacles needed to be the most important aspect of each card design. Throughout the rest of the Minor Arcana, my imagination would have to evolve harmoniously alongside the pips in order for each card to be successful.

I created the gothic building pictured in the Eight of Swords from a composite of photos taken of the Cathedral of the Incarnation in Garden City, New York (shown left).

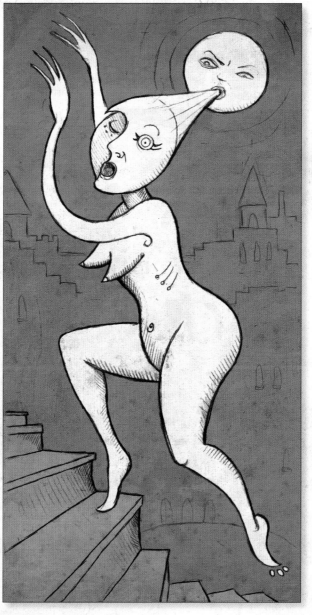

Sketch (2006)

Seven of Swords

A masked harlequin attempts to swallow his swords in a dramatic display of skill. He contorts his long body into a precarious position, balancing a heavy sword across his feet while another sword dangles on a rope above his wide-open mouth. More concerned with his flashy appearance, the harlequin rushes to perform before he is competent in his art. He has one foot twisted backwards while the other is bare, suggesting that he is not quite prepared to execute such a daring act. Regardless, the impulsive harlequin continues his risky performance, even though his plans are seriously flawed. The frayed rope, which binds the two blades above him, will soon break, leaving him in a tragic predicament.

Three swords stand stabbed into the ground, representing past failures. Although the harlequin has tried this stunt before, he has not learned from his mistakes. He continues to do things the way he always has, and wonders why he always gets the same miserable results. At his side lie two swords that he hopes to use successfully in the future. They will be failures as well if the foolish harlequin does not modify his technique. With fingers crossed, he relies on luck more than a sound strategy.

Upright meanings:

Don't make a fool of yourself! An ill-conceived plan is about to lead you directly down a path of failure. Like the reckless harlequin, you may be putting yourself at risk due to a lack of foresight. Know that your hasty actions will only bring ruin to all that you've strived for. Furthermore, you must not become overconfident. You may be overlooking vital details and ignoring danger in your hurry to achieve a spectacular outcome. It is unwise to presume that all will work out by chance alone. Take the time needed to review your ideas and be flexible enough to make crucial adjustments.

Reversed meanings:

Don't be deterred by setbacks! You will need to make many attempts before you attain the positive result you desire. Although your undertakings may have failed before, there is a way to succeed, provided you are willing to try something radically new. Be persistent and keep your goal foremost in your mind. Through trial and error, you will eventually realize your ambitions in a unique and astonishing way.

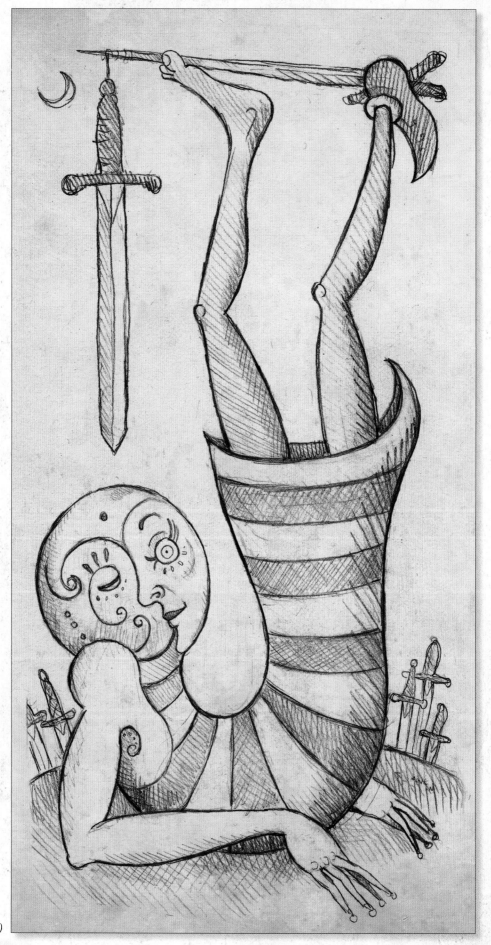

Sketch (2006)

THE ACROBAT

Many of the characters found in the Deviant Moon deck developed from inconsequential scribbles made over the years. When I began to design the Seven of Swords, I immediately thought of an old crayon sketch I had made more than two decades earlier. The drawing portrayed a little acrobat performing a balancing act with balls, strings and sticks. Like many other neglected and forgotten characters, this one demanded a role in the Deviant Moon Tarot as well, although he needed to undergo a few changes first. As the final variation of the card progressed, the acrobat eventually evolved into a sword-swallowing harlequin. However, he never lost his playful essence or his twisted foot in the transformation.

"The Acrobat" (1982?)

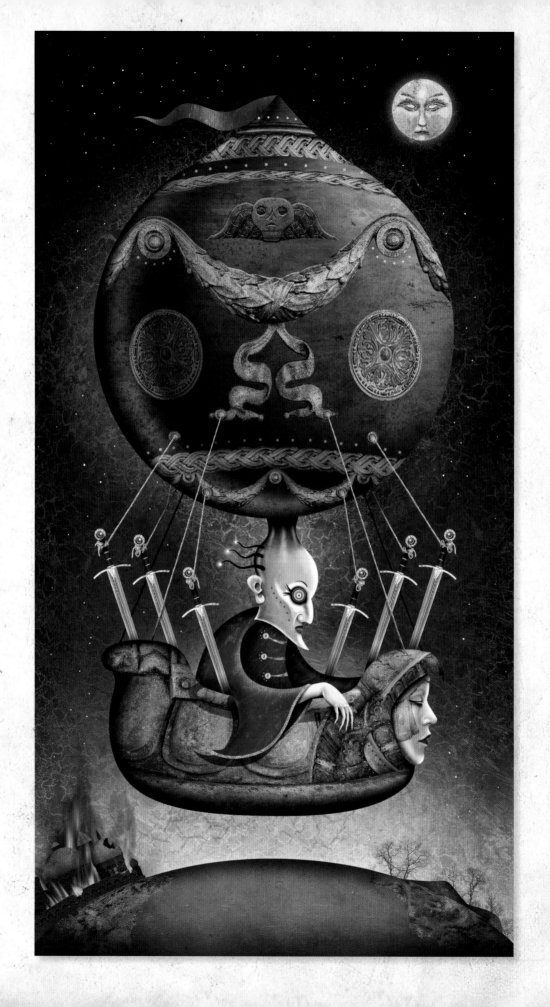

Six of Swords

Internal conflicts have left the Kingdom of Swords in ruins. Castles burn and blood runs through the streets as the hostile citizens take up arms against one another. A lone resident, wishing to escape the unrest, dares to imagine himself rising above the turmoil. Uplifting thoughts inflate his mind and manifest into an enormous balloon at the top of his head. As the refugee ascends into the sky, he gains a new perspective on the world, for the objects on the ground no longer obscure opportunity. From this altitude, he can finally see his unexplored destiny in the distance. With his future goals now in sight, the refugee journeys over the ocean, setting the course of his own life with steadfast determination.

Curious symbolism covers the airship. On the bow, we see the profile of a veiled figurehead. Her subconscious intuition serves to guide the refugee through the darkness of night. Funerary markings decorate the outside of the balloon. This could mean that the refugee has found a way to use his morbid thoughts to his advantage. In spite of his nightmares he excels by concentrating on lofty ideas, and by refusing to be consumed by his troubled origins. Six swords also aid in the creation of this escape vehicle, showing that the voyager has overcome pain and hardship by utilizing his ingenuity. Although he must carry these blades to new lands, he does not think of them as a burden. They have become part of his character and his enlightened journey would be impossible without them.

Even though the airship has broken free from the anarchy on the ground, there is still much turbulence swirling through the air. The direction of the red flag waving on top of the balloon indicates that the craft is traveling against the wind. Above, the deviant moon tries to deflate the traveler's high ambitions, using subliminal taunts and discouraging vibrations. Undeterred by the resistance, the refugee moves forward, considering no other option but the successful realization of his dreams.

Upright meanings:

Rise up and transcend your chaotic mental state! The Six of Swords encourages you to think your way out of volatile situations and discover the tranquility you desire. Set high standards, and do not allow yourself to be grounded by negativity. It is vital that you make the mental shift from destructive to empowering thought patterns. Solve problems creatively, and let your boundless imagination lift you to new heights. By using your intellectual power, you can turn adversity and misfortune into a means of achieving success.

Reversed meanings:

When reversed, the Six of Swords says that you may have difficulty breaking free from dire circumstances. You might be trapped in a destructive setting simply because you cannot envision yourself rising above the pandemonium surrounding you. Understand that your aspirations will never take flight if you focus on problems instead of solutions.

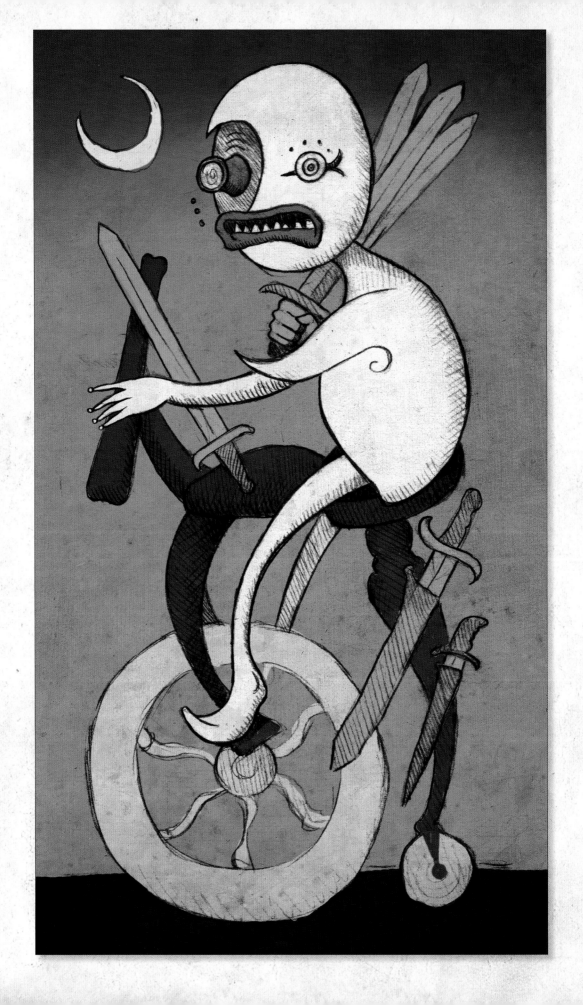

COMPOSITION COLLISION

Many ideas for the cards came about through accidental discoveries. For example, while creating the Six of Swords, I found that the head of the citizen and the burners of the balloon competed for the same space in the composition. There was no room for either of them to work successfully in the design without ruining the proportion of the other. It seemed as if they wanted to blend as one, and were stubbornly resisting all attempts to keep them apart. After taking the advice of my subconscious, I simply joined the balloon to the top of the citizen's head. This finally solved the composition problem while unintentionally making the entire image much more profound.

The initial design for the Six of Swords showed an egg-headed creature riding his strange bicycle around the kingdom (left). Photographical sources for this piece were to come from cracked eggshells, bones and insect parts. More than likely, this rejected character will appear in a future project.

FIVE OF SWORDS

A trusted general from the king's army has turned traitor. In his betrayal, he has given sensitive information to the enemy, which was used to defeat the king on the battlefield. A white flag waves meekly from atop a tower signaling the city's surrender.

Gloating over this underhanded victory, the two-faced general openly mocks the citizens for having such an inept leader. Although the general may have outwitted the king, his deceit makes his triumph a complete travesty.

Seething with sarcasm, the general pompously enters the castle courtyard and unleashes a barrage of insults upon the royal family. Spitting his sharp tongue from his foul mouth, he lashes the king with obscenities. He proceeds to collect five swords surrendered to him off the ground. Casually, he rests two blades over his shoulder, snickering to himself over the apparent ease of his success. Another sword stands defiantly stabbed into the ground and will not be taken so easily. Two more blades lay crossed on the floor, waiting to be picked up. They represent the continuation of conflict between the general and the king in the future.

Realizing the type of foe he faces, the wise king chooses not to retaliate at this time. His submissive response is not a sign of weakness, but merely a strategic ploy. For now, he will endure the affronts for the sake of his kingdom, and patiently wait until he knows more about his devious challenger before striking back.

Upright meanings:

Take a close look at your friendships. If the Five of Swords happens to swagger its way into your reading, it could mean that someone you trust may be out to do you harm. This person will revel in your defeat and ridicule you when you're down. Those you confide in might expose your secrets in a despicable manner. Liars might cheat you out of what is rightfully yours and double-cross you. Incredibly, these swindlers will blatantly brag about their misconduct! They will steal your ideas and take credit for your hard-earned accomplishments. Although you might feel stripped of all dignity, you must realize that now is not the time to seek revenge. Accept your loss and learn from this setback. Study your opponent first and then make an intelligent comeback.

On the other hand, you may be the victor in a given situation, but this might have come about through trickery and dishonest actions. Beware! The negative energy you have created will soon find its way back to you. Keep in mind that your arrogance will lead to your downfall.

When the Five of Swords appears upside down, it is a sure sign that a false friend might be exposed. Treacherous plots against you will be uncovered and foiled. Rumors and lies will be proven untrue. In this position, the card can also imply that a quarrel or feud will soon end, as the parties involved tire of conflict.

THE SPECTRAL SOLDIER

When I was a boy, sleep-induced apparitions often visited me in the middle of the night. One of the most colorful specters to appear in my bedroom was a feeble-minded revolutionary war soldier. He wore a tattered uniform and looked as though he had been dead for a very long time. The soldier sometimes appeared on the side of my bed, mumbling to himself and rubbing his hand over the large crack in his head, while his white, lifeless eyes stared into oblivion. Confused, he would stumble around my room in the dark looking for something inside my closet he never could seem to find. I can still see his ponytail bobbing up and down behind his skull as he waddled about in search of his lost belongings.

As the years went on, the phantom soldier eventually stopped his nocturnal visits. Although I have yet to encounter his presence again, his lasting influence helped me design the treacherous general seen on this card, as well as the skeletal soldier found on the Two of Cups.

"The Defeated Soldier Solemnly Gathers the Swords of his Fallen Comrades off of the Battlefield", early sketch (2006)

FOUR OF SWORDS

The girl in the ground is dreaming again. Vivid visions run through her mind and illuminate the tips of her braided hair. These powerful subconscious thoughts fill her grave with an energy that keeps four funeral roses in bloom around her. The flowers represent memories of life; the joy of what was and the pity of what will never be.

Withdrawn and alone, the little girl is the queen of solitude. Though her limbs appear crossed in a postmortem position, she is far from dead. She merely rests, undisturbed by the bustle of life, in a timeless state of hibernation. With her body embedded in an ocean of dirt, she can safely immerse herself in imagination rather than participate in a turbulent childhood. Like a newly planted seed, she waits for the proper conditions to sprout up and grow to maturity. As the cocoon of soil nourishes her essence, we see the wispy glow of an angelic metamorphosis beginning to take place.

As dawn approaches, the crescent moon prepares to dip below the horizon in silence. Meanwhile, the desolate field below struggles to keep its secret hidden. Three swords have been plunged into the ground with tremendous force, marking the site of the girl's lonely resting place. This shows that she was buried under troubled circumstances, and has painfully departed from the world above. A fourth sword lies buried beside her, symbolizing the anguish that follows her even in retreat. Her mind will change the meaning of this terrible sword through thoughtful meditation, and she will use its cutting blade to her advantage when she resurfaces.

UPRIGHT MEANINGS:

Bury yourself in thought! Collect your ideas together and contemplate in peaceful surroundings. Realize that the mental clarity you seek can only be achieved through isolation. Eliminate distractions and reconnect with your inner self. Through quiet reflection, you will be able to hear the subtle vibrations of your spirit and transcend all earthly limitations.

The Four of Swords can also mean that you need to take a break. Like the child, you may be feeling a strong urge to escape your problems and worries. Give yourself time to recharge by shutting off from the daily stress of life. Get some sleep and rejuvenate. You will experience strong growth during an extended period of rest, which will enable you to face a tough situation in the near future.

An adverse interpretation of this card might warn of banishment from friends or society. This could come about through imprisonment or by going into exile. During such seclusion, it would be wise to ponder the true purpose of your existence.

The Four of Swords in reverse calls you to return to daily life. Wake up, dust yourself off, and get moving again! Reemerge into the world and resume projects and activities with passion. In this position, the card may also be warning you not to rest, even though you are fatigued or burnt out. You must keep up the momentum, without pause. A break at this point could lead to failure.

The Girl in the Ground

The girl in the ground was inspired by a legend floating around my elementary school back in the mid 1970s. Children whispered of a little girl murdered and buried in the schoolyard more than fifty years before. Her alleged name was Phyllis Lancaster. Although no one knew where her supposed burial spot was, my friends and I believed she was under the grass of the school baseball field, just behind third base. When playing ball, we all ran a little bit quicker past this spot, believing Phyllis might reach up through the dirt and grab our ankles with her bony fingers.

A piece torn from a blanket was used to create the girl's tattered clothing. It was buried for weeks and then left out in the rain to give it the ragged effect I was looking for.

"The Girl in the Ground is Dreaming Again" (2002), left

THREE OF SWORDS

Asorrowful woman stands alone in her chamber, betrayed and abandoned by love. Three swords stab her from behind, marking the treacherous deeds inflicted by someone she once trusted. As the sharp blades pierce the woman's heart, they leave a blood-red stain of despair on her clothing. Cautiously, she touches the pointed metal tips with her finger, trying to determine if the pain she feels is real or imagined.

Though she is in agony, the woman makes no effort to remove the terrible swords from her body. Instead, she allows herself to be victimized and cornered by misery. Her three legs show that she is stable enough to withstand the heartache and that she could walk away from this sad situation at any time. Choosing to stay put and suffer, she waits by an open window for an approaching electrical storm to bring more turbulence into her life. If she is not careful, the metal sticking out of her chest will attract dangerous lighting, which might strike her dead with a thunderous bolt.

Reality shines its spotlight on the woman, yet she dramatically turns her head away in self-pity and denial rather than face the truth of her situation. Depressing thoughts blacken the hand she uses to shield her forehead from the bright light. The woeful pose she strikes casts an exaggerated shadow against the wall behind her, making her anguished feelings loom larger than life. Even though her eyes are all cried out, the distraught woman manages to squeeze out one last teardrop, which slithers like a lonely black slug down the side of her cheek.

Upright meanings:

The Three of Swords symbolizes a period of severe heartache. Tragedy overshadows all you could be happy for. It's a wonder you are still standing in light of the sadness, which lacerates your soul. Everything around you leads you to believe that you are hopelessly stuck in an unending state of grief. Although events beyond your control have darkened your mood, you must realize that you are the one in control of your emotions!

The origin of this unwarranted pain can come from a variety of possible sources. You might be suffering over the absence or loss of a loved one. In this time of mourning, awful feelings of separation seem unbearable. Thoughts of those you miss will likely dominate your mind and upset your spirit. Perhaps you feel unable to exist without them.

The Three of Swords might tell of a romantic break up ending in disaster, or of a disloyal friend who has betrayed your confidence. Such hurtful events will leave you feeling as if your tender heart has been impaled by cold steel. Infidelity could be another way to interpret this gloomy card. A lover's deception may be revealed, bringing irreconcilable mistrust into the relationship. On the other hand, maybe you are the one causing distress to another through

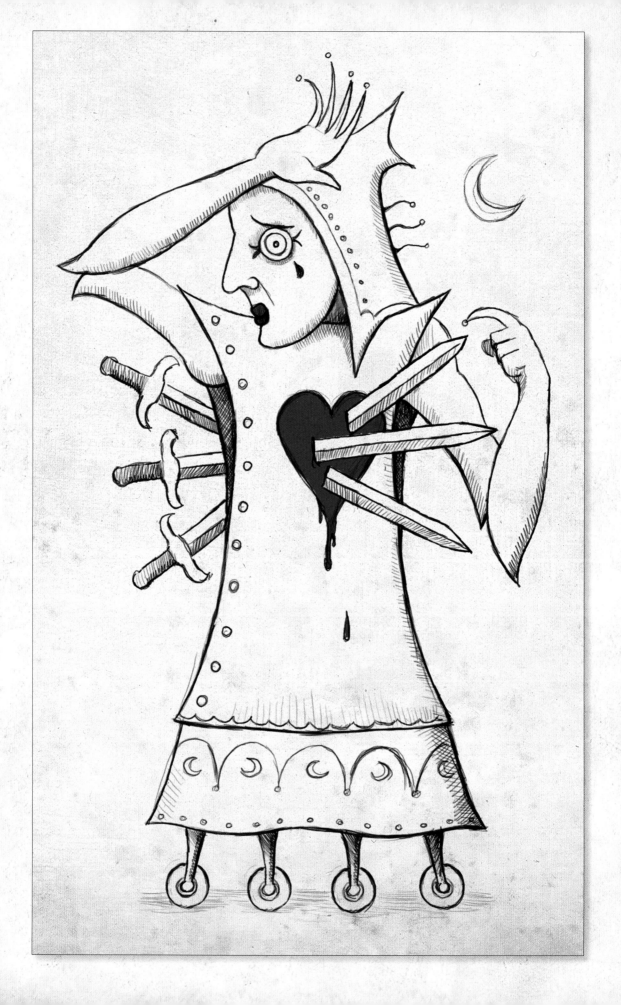

your deceptive and unfaithful actions. This card may also mean that a stormy or violent relationship is looming overhead. Instead of love, all you receive from this abusive bond is heart-wrenching pain and mental anguish.

REVERSED MEANINGS:

Take heart! Your injured emotions are on the healing path. In this position, the Three of Swords suggests that you are ready to move on with life after an extremely sorrowful event or a great loss. The time has come to accept the harsh reality of what has happened, regardless of how wrong or unfair it might have been. Gather your wounded love and carry on, but leave those hurtful swords behind. Although there may be tears left to cry, and your damaged soul still aches, find comfort in knowing that the dark clouds have parted, revealing a radiant morning sky ahead.

In initial sketches, the sorrowful woman resembled a royal character from a playing card. I felt the clothing from this design would be too colorful and ornate for the solemn feeling I wished to convey, so I had her change into something drabber for the occasion. The face in this drawing later went on to become the worried expression of the old woman in the Nine of Swords.

Two of Swords

A mighty, two-headed swordsman stands motionless in the castle courtyard, resembling an unbreakable stone statue. The internal conflict he has waged against himself has resulted in stalemate, with neither the light nor the dark side of his body being able to overpower the will of the other. Frustrated by the lack of progress in his battle, the divided warrior uses this respite to reevaluate his tactics before his warring halves clash again. With swords crossed at the hilt, both sides rest their blades over their shoulders in a guarded position while carefully looking for weakness in their opponent. Tension builds as the dual minds knock together and stare each other down without blinking. In silence, they wait to see who will strike first, yet neither wants to disrupt the unexpected balance brought about by their struggle. From above, the moon mediates the equilibrium by sending beams of calm energy into their thoughts, hoping to turn this fragile truce into a sustainable era of peace.

Upright meanings:

If you run up against the Two of Swords, it could represent an area in your life that has reached an impasse. Your advancement is being blocked by what seems to be an immovable obstacle. The harder you push, the harder it pushes back! Strenuous contests will end in a draw as opposing forces become deadlocked. Be advised that you are butting heads with a challenger whose skill equals your own. This person thinks as you do, and foresees your every move. Remember, if you keep performing the same actions, you will always achieve the same results. To gain the upper hand, you need to throw your rival off balance by surprising him with an innovative maneuver.

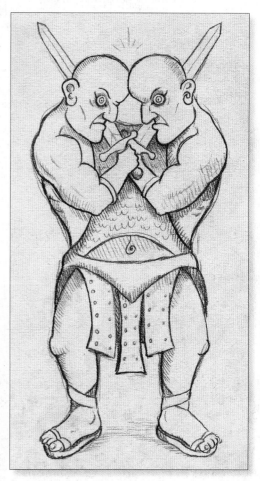

Reversed meanings:

Make up your mind! In reverse, this card shows that you are unable to decide between two difficult choices. Know that such indecision stalls your ambitions. Do not be afraid to break your predictable line of thinking. Evaluate the negative possibilities versus the positive. Then come up with a third option, and set yourself up to win.

The matching tattoos on the swordsman's shoulders show that both his dark and light sides have similar aspirations. In order for the swordsman to realize his true potential, he must stop being his own worst enemy and unite his warring halves into a single force.

Pencil sketch (2006)

ACE OF SWORDS

The majestic archangel guards her mind against the onslaught of deception. With steadfast courage, she stands her ground and displays the virtue of her noble sword. The double-edged blade she wields has been forged by her inner spirit, and serves not only to defend her convictions, but to lash out in offense as well. The angel places the weapon alongside her head, showing that her fortitude is derived from her mental powers. Her vibrant thoughts flow through the blade and strengthen the steel, causing the sharp tip to glow with intense energy. Although her determination is unwavering, the angel must keep a vigilant watch over the growth of self-doubt. Like a wild vine, it seeks to entangle itself around her upright sword, and slowly creep into her dreams.

On top of the angel's head sits a flourishing crown of ivy. The succulent, green leaves symbolize her ability to bring bold new ideas to life by blending confidence with intelligence. Jutting through the garland, glorious spikes of gold rise up like the morning sun, representing the awakening of the angel's brilliant potential.

In the background, the moon quietly drifts away into the distant sky. Its subliminal influence is weak against the angel's resolve to liberate her thoughts and control her own mind. With open wings, the clear-thinking archangel is free to fly as far as she can envision.

Upright meanings:

Feel the awesome power of the Ace of Swords rising up inside you! Your indomitable spirit will unite with your mind, becoming a razor sharp force for good. As your conscience bursts with new insights, it will become increasingly difficult for you to sit idly by and ignore the rampant spread of inequity in your life. Uphold your principles and defend your rights. Now is the time to turn your energetic thoughts into heroic action. You may be summoned to champion a moral cause in a quest to expose the truth and challenge injustice. Be brave, and do not fear taking the fight to the enemy. By focusing on a cause, you will be able to cut intimidating problems down to size, and triumph over adversity.

Reversed meanings:

Misguided logic distorts your sense of priority! When the Ace of Swords appears on its head, it indicates that your mental focus is weak, dull and fragmented. In this state of confusion, it will become difficult to defend or assert your beliefs. Aggressors could trample your dignity unopposed while a timid spirit quivers within you. You might also be planning vengeance against an offender with no thought of the possible consequences.

Preliminary sketch (2006)

The angel depicted in the Ace of Swords is a close relative of the angel found on the Temperance card. Both of them combine different elements together to create something dynamically new and unique. While one creates harmony with her mix, the other blends willpower with brainpower, often to advance a philosophical agenda. The latter combination may be volatile if not channeled properly, and can lead to extremism. The portrayal of a temperate angel lends moderation to the ideological ambitions of the ace.

This early sketch shows the angel in profile wearing a lunar costume. I did not use this design because I felt a frontal view would better convey her self-assured attitude and make the card more confrontational. This composition later became the basis of design for the Ace of Cups.

Suit of Wands

The energetic members of the Tribe of Wands live their lives with passion and creativity. Through their inspired endeavors, they seek to achieve personal growth and realize their potential. These fearless individuals are willing to take bold risks when pursuing their dreams; however, at times they begin without a sound strategy. When faced with problems or setbacks, they use their ingenious imagination to overcome hardships. They know that success requires disciplined effort and that they are responsible for their own destiny.

King of Wands

Those looking for the King of Wands will not find him chained to a sedentary throne. Tonight he is outside walking with his children, leading them on an exciting adventure through the woods. The demands of the kingdom will have to wait until he returns, for there is nothing more important to the King than spending time with his family.

On this current expedition, the intrepid King escorts his youngsters along an unfamiliar trail. The uncertainty of the trip is thrilling to the children. They chatter incessantly about the possible discoveries that lie ahead, fully trusting in their father's guidance. The King marks the progress of the hike by firmly stamping his staff into the ground after each step. His confident moves convey a sense of stability to the children at his side. Topping his staff is a large amber diamond, which soaks up the energy of this pleasurable evening.

The children quicken their pace and hurry to keep up with their father's long strides. One child affectionately latches onto the King's back for a ride, while another holds the King's hand so as not to fall behind and become lost. A third child has stopped walking to tug at his father's royal robe and ask a question about the journey. This child is darker than his siblings are, and may not be a blood relation to the King. His presence could signify the blending of two families through marriage, or that he is an adopted son. Regardless of the situation, the King clearly loves the boy as his own flesh.

The crescent moon hovering in the sky expresses the positive influence the King has on his children's subconscious. When the children grow up and go out on their own, their father's wisdom will echo in their minds even if he is no longer physically there to shepherd them through life.

The King of Wands wears a crown of upturned roots through which he absorbs mental nourishment from the universe above.

Upright meanings:

The King of Wands represents a charismatic leader who inspires others to explore their own greatness. Like the King, you must rally your flock and courageously guide them through uncharted territories. The people you oversee admire your energetic style and regard you as a role model. Motivate them with the strength of your character, and always set excellent examples for them to follow. Be attentive to their varied needs. If you support others' dreams, they will enthusiastically support your dreams as well.

Reversed meanings:

In reverse, the King of Wands may represent an intolerant leader who has unreasonable expectations of others. He desires everyone to worship the ground he walks on, yet he will tread on his followers as he goes. Like him, you might be managing others with your callous ego. Be mindful not to overstep your bounds with those who trust and depend on you.

An inverted King of Wands could refer to a strict or cruel parent. This selfish person often ignores his children and leaves them alone to fend for themselves. In this position, the card might also allude to unruly youngsters in need of stable parental supervision.

Finally, the reversed King might indicate your desire to regain control and change the direction of your life. You may try to go out and pursue your calling; however, the weighty demands of others will impede your progress.

Many characters in the suit of Wands carry a small piece of amber with them as they make their way through life. This tells of their ability to convert negative energy into positive results. Like them, I have been carrying my own piece of amber around in my pocket since adolescence. For unknown reasons, I have always felt cheerful when rubbing the smooth surface of the polished amber between my fingers. Sometimes, I hold the golden stone up to the sun, let it absorb the magnificence of the day, and trap memories like insects inside for eternity.

"Tree Boy", sketch (2007), far left

Rough sketch (2007), top right

"Leaf Boy", sketch (2007), bottom right

Queen of Wands

The confident Queen of Wands stands as a dominant personality in the forest. She is a formidable warrior who inspires her tribe to be strong and courageous. Like a hunter, she will relentlessly pursue her desires regardless of the obstacles. However, she sometimes resorts to more gentle tactics when confronted by a stubborn opponent. In such instances, she uses her irresistible charm to persuade her rivals into becoming lifelong allies.

The card pictures the Queen proudly holding her royal spear, the pointed tip of which crosses over the full moon. This is symbolic of the power she derives by combining sharp intellect with intuition. Passionate ideas grow out of her head and twist into flaming strands of auburn hair. The intense color ignites the autumn air with excitement and captivates the attention of everyone she meets.

The Queen's physical appearance reveals much about her character. For example, one can clearly see that nature has endowed her with four arms. This inherent gift gives her the capability to take on multiple roles and responsibilities. One might also notice that her muscular leg sticks out from behind her leafy sarong. This implies her readiness to leap into action, although some may interpret this as a form of enticement.

The Queen does not cover herself in elegant or expensive material. Unlike other women of her stature, she wears an organic dress created from dried leaves and sticks. Draped across her chest is a thin leather strap. It marks an area on her torso where a second pair of breasts once was. Some say the Queen removed her breast to increase her effectiveness in combat. This act of self-sacrifice demonstrates her willingness to forgo a bit of flesh to better fight for her convictions.

A large amber orb hangs on the belt below the Queen's navel, which may be a sign that she is trying to conceive. When it comes to mothering, the Queen trains her offspring to be self-reliant. She emboldens them to fight back when hurt and refuses to offer sympathy. The Queen knows that her children must be tough to survive in the forest.

Upright meanings:

The Queen of Wands personifies feminine strength and fortitude. Let her assertive qualities inspire you to take action on your creative ideas. Be assured in your ability to achieve greatness. Know that you are competent enough to deal with any difficulty you might encounter.

The Queen of Wands is someone who thinks for herself. She is fiercely independent and does not need the King or anyone else to validate her worth. Follow her example and summon the courage to express your opinions to the world. Although others may

try to suppress your noble ambitions, you should not allow yourself to remain in a socially submissive role. Like the Queen, you must stand tall and seize command of your own affairs.

The Queen of Wands might also signify the presence of a well-liked and attractive female in your life. This venerated woman is popular in many circles. Her lively energy spreads like wildfire amongst all she meets. Do whatever it takes to get in her good favor, for she holds tremendous power over your destiny.

Reversed meanings:

When standing on her head, the Queen of Wands becomes a vindictive character, bent on seeking revenge. She hunts for negative attention in an attempt to make herself feel important. This bossy person will try to manipulate all with her inflated ego. She demands admiration from others but offers nothing in return. Sex is often her weapon of choice, and she will cold-heartedly use it to further her ambitions.

In this position, the card can also represent a timid female who lacks the confidence to pursue her dreams aggressively. This person may have been prominent at one time, but her popularity has long since waned.

Queen of Wands, ink sketch from an abandoned deck

An early sketch of a rotund queen made of flower petals and blossoms, left

Knight of Wands

The daring Knight of Wands scurries across a grassy field fused to the back of a colossal flea. The flea serves as a workhorse while the Knight is the mastermind. Together, they venture out into the unknown as a combined force, ready to confront life's challenges. The full moon rising in the background is symbolic of the satisfaction they will achieve by aggressively chasing a dream and fighting for its realization.

The Knight uses the flea as a means to leap quickly over vast distances, while keeping his own delicate wings in pristine condition. This shows that he leverages his relationships and conserves his talents for what matters most. Although the Knight is in command of the flea, its behavior can be erratic. The flea sometimes jumps too far and carries the Knight way beyond his intended destination. They often miss their mark because they never stop bouncing long enough to evaluate their position or formulate a strategy of attack.

The Knight clutches his thorny wand and prepares for combat. He wears the green exoskeleton of a mantis as armor, which not only protects him, but also serves to intimidate his opponents. The only visible hint of his humanity is the lower portion of his face. His open mouth yells out a battle call, warning the world to stand aside or deal with his fury.

Like a mantis, the Knight is a formidable hunter who usually gets whatever he goes after. He is fearless in his pursuits and outwardly displays his passion, yet the flea on which he rides is unthinking and void of emotion. This repulsive creature is a carrier of death, and its skull portends the devastation it brings to its enemies. The mere sight of the flea stirs primordial terror in the hearts of the bravest warriors. Each time it infests a new area its tongue slithers out of its mouth to sample the atmosphere, hoping to detect potential prey.

The Knight is swift to adapt to changing circumstances. When the flea no longer suits his needs, he will coldly detach himself from it to join with some other entity.

Upright meanings:

The Knight of Wands represents someone who enthusiastically takes the initiative. This action-oriented person is quick to pounce on new and exciting opportunities, and often makes spontaneous decisions. Like him, you must saddle up and get moving on your creative ideas. Let nothing prevent you from seizing your destiny!

The Knight's greatest shortcoming is that he sometimes does not think before leaping into action. Although he has a strong desire to succeed, he may fail in what he sets out to achieve due to his impulsivity and lack of foresight. He will become an unstoppable

powerhouse once he discovers how to match his bold ambition with sound planning and patience.

The Knight exudes raging sexual energy. Unfortunately, the inability to contain his lustful desires may lead to his downfall. His appearance in a reading might signify someone who uses another person for a quick sexual encounter, recklessly hopping from partner to partner.

The Knight of Wands may also signify military personnel or someone seeking adventure in a foreign land.

Reversed meanings:

When reversed, the Knight of Wands could indicate that you have lost your sense of direction in life. This is because you are squandering your time and energy on activities that lead you away from your higher purpose. Although you may be off course, remember that you are ultimately in control and have the power to turn yourself around whenever you want.

In this position, the card might warn of delayed or disrupted plans. Expect to feel frustration and anger as unfortunate circumstances derail your momentum. Do not let your ill-tempered emotions keep you from reaching your goal. Despite any setback, you must compose yourself and get back on track straightaway.

Preliminary sketch (2007)

"Flying Knight", early sketch (2007), left

Page of Wands

The young Page of Wands has journeyed far from his springtime home and into an unfamiliar realm of frost. Here, there are no flowers to applaud his efforts or birds to sing him a welcoming song. Most members of his tribe would have turned back at the first sight of snow, but the eager Page presses onward with excitement. Guided by curiosity, he explores this strange land and marvels at its wintry wonders.

The Page soon comes face to face with what seems to be an impassable obstacle. A frozen pond lies before him, and the cracking ice looks thin. The Page could easily get to the other side by going around the pond, but safety is not foremost on his youthful mind. Deciding to take the adventurous route, he constructs a pair of stilts out of two small tree trunks and boldly uses them to trek across the treacherous pond. He is confident that he can avoid danger as long as his feet do not touch the ice. Remarkably, tender green leaves sprout from the wood, symbolizing the freshness of this novel approach.

The frozen trees in the distance expect to see the Page collapse through the fragile ice. Their chilled whispers fill the air with doubt, but the Page is the child of a different season and does not relate to such skepticism. He personifies the newness of spring and budding ingenuity. His leafy green attire contrasts with the silvery world around him. When others see only winter, he visualizes warmer days yet to come. He believes in his potential and is willing to put his ideas to the test.

In the card, the crossed stilts form an "X", which means that the Page has reached a defining moment in his journey. His daring excursion will either turn out successful or end in catastrophe. He must keep moving steadily across the pond, for if he stops to rethink his plan, his static weight will break the ice below and he will fall into a freezing pool of death. Regardless of the possible outcomes, the Page remains undaunted by the inherent risks of his actions. The combination of naivety and faith might be all that the Page needs to overcome the impossible.

Upright meanings:

When the innocent Page of Wands passes through your reading, he brings along his childlike imagination and creativity. Like him, you must confront life's difficulties with youthful optimism and energy. Examine your problems from a fresh perspective and then try something unheard of. Think differently! Avoid routine traditions and do something exciting for a change. Be resourceful and find new ways to make things happen. Take action before you have all the answers. Stay confident knowing that innovative solutions will present themselves as you go. Do not be discouraged if others consider your strategy impractical or foolish. Keep in mind that your cockamamie scheme just might work! All you have to do is stick to your inspired plan and see it through to the end. Know that outstanding rewards wait on the other side.

The appearance of the Page of Wands in a reading may also represent a young genius or talented prodigy.

"Bird Boy", early sketch (2007)

Reversed meanings:

When reversed, the Page of Wands warns that you are walking on thin ice in regards to an important issue. Proceed with caution! The stability in your life can shatter at any moment. Realize that you are stuck in the middle of this precarious situation because of foolish planning. You have been lucky up until now, however you have failed to consider the consequences of your actions. The time has come to pay the price for your risky behavior and stupidity. Brace yourself for a potential disaster.

In this position, the card might also indicate that you are terrified to try something different. Perhaps you lack self-confidence in your abilities. You could be justifying your inaction by telling yourself that the risk is not worth the reward. In your mind, it is better to play it safe than to do something you may regret later on. Realize that your dreams are getting colder while you sit frozen in fear along the sidelines.

Posing for the Page of Wands

My daughter patiently posed as a model for numerous characters in the deck. As we worked together, she would offer her own suggestions on how each citizen might stand or handle an object. She also helped color coordinate many of their costumes. She would take one look at the artwork and let me know if someone's jacket mismatched his pants, or if I should use a better shade of blue for the queen's royal dress. Her young advice was spot-on every time and invaluable to the creation of the deck.

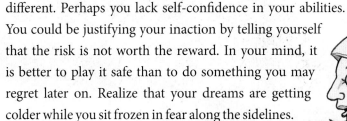

"Boy on Stilts", early sketch (2007)

179

Ten of Wands

An overburdened woodsman slowly makes his way home after a long day's labor. He plods along a weary path, barely clinging to ten wands gathered from the forest. The crushing weight of the bundle in his tired arms almost brings the woodsman to his knees. Although he struggles, his abilities are sufficient to manage this heavy load.

One can look at this card and interpret the woodsman's plight as being either positive or negative. In the positive version, the woodsman harvests his success day by day and slowly accumulates greatness. He is willing to exert tremendous effort now because he knows that he will reap finer rewards in the future. Each load he carries brings him closer to achieving his vision of a better life. In the distance, the full moon shines brightly in the warm autumn sky. It reminds the woodsman to think of the satisfaction he will attain once his labor is complete.

The negative connotation implies that the woodsman is a slave to the grind. He toils to fulfill the desires and aspirations of others, but derives little reward from his efforts. The dry wands he carries are dead and bear no leaves. This could mean that he feels no passion for his work or considers it unimaginative. The woodsman is resentful of the workload but does little to alter his course. The daily pressure he endures has hardened him to the point of being unrecognizable to his loved ones. Life seems like a burden to him, and he is on the verge of losing his grip.

In either case, the woodsman's bundle is essential to his survival; however, his method of transport is not efficient. He would do well to work smarter instead of harder, and use his brain as well as his brawn. He cannot go on with this backbreaking routine without putting himself in an early grave. He needs to rest for a moment and figure out a better way to do his job. For example, he could use some of his wood to build a small wagon and easily double the load he carries now. If he traded those extra loads for a horse and carriage, he could multiply his results tenfold.

The woodsman purposely left his prized axe behind in the forest. He knew that if he took the axe with him, the extra weight would have made his cumbersome load impossible to carry. The lesson here is that sometimes it is necessary to sacrifice something valuable in order to facilitate a hefty dream.

Upright meanings:

In the tarot, the number ten indicates that a phase in your life has ended. With this in mind, the Ten of Wands may be a sign that your hard work is about to pay off and will soon no longer be necessary. Get set to enjoy the fruits of your labor! Retirement may be just around the bend.

Perhaps you are struggling with a difficult project. Know that this exhausting task can only be finished through long hours of intense labor. Discipline yourself to do what is uncomfortable. Do not expect success without struggle.

The Ten of Wands could also mean that you have taken on too much and have reached your personal limit. Overwhelming responsibility weighs heavy on your shoulders, while stress, worry and fear burden your mind. Always remember that you possess the strength to handle whatever life brings.

Additionally, the card might represent a workaholic or an overworked person. Maybe you are toiling under oppressive working conditions with little or no relief in sight. Realize that this is taking its toll on your physical and mental well-being.

Reversed meanings:

In reverse, the Ten of Wands suggests that you eliminate inessential tasks and responsibilities from your daily life. Stop trying to hold on to more than you can control. Let go of low-value activities and concentrate on your most important priorities. Leave your pride behind and ask someone for help. Know that you will accomplish more in less time if you delegate some of your duties. Take a break from your drudgery and start planning a long-overdue vacation.

In this position, the card might also indicate that you feel unfulfilled by your current occupation. The hard work you are doing seems meaningless and barely worth the effort. Rid yourself of this lifeless job and redirect your energy toward work that moves you closer to your goals!

"An Old Shrew Cooking a Pot of Goulash" (Five of Cups)

Sketches of various Trollious citizens (1981, Age 14)

"The Architect" (Forerunner to the Magician)

"Opinder and his Miniature Buildings"

"An Edler Statesman"
(Boots borrowed by the Emperor)

"Oil Wagon Pulled by a Red Bull"

I wanted to give the woodsman a cantankerous look to show how his strenuous life had affected him. After doing a few sketches, I chose to portray him as a burley avian creature instead of a "normal" looking citizen. Inspiration for this birdman came from a drawing I made in my early teens. The drawing depicts four sailors resembling pelicans working hard to unload coffins from a cargo ship. I can imagine these creatures cursing and grumbling with each black box they carry to shore. Interestingly enough, one of the sailors accidentally drops his mysterious shipment and spills the dead body of a woman onto the dock.

"Spilled Secrets", watercolor sketch (1981, Age 14)

THE TROLLIOUS

When I was 12 years old, I developed a strange breed of avian people called the "Trollious." They were the predecessors to the Deviant Moon and its citizens. They too had stylized circular eyes, and they even wore similar costumes. I used to draw these medieval characters on brown paper bags to give the illustrations an antiquated feel. In fact, one of my initial childhood designs for a tarot deck featured the Trollious in all their glory. Unfortunately, those early tarot designs no longer exist, however, a few of my old paper bag drawings still survive. These drawings clearly show how the Trollious influenced the creation of the Deviant Moon Tarot.

"A Trollious Knight"

Nine of Wands

A masked boy has found himself trapped inside of an underground labyrinth. Exploring endless tunnels and climbing winding stairs was fun for him at first, but as he ventured deeper into the maze it slowly turned into a prison. After searching in vain for an exit, he is beginning to believe that escape is impossible. Discouraged and tired, he crawls onto a high ledge and rests. As the weary boy dangles his bare feet over the abyss below, he considers giving in to his bleak fate.

Ivy vines creep into the labyrinth, showing that the outside world is near. Similar signs of salvation are all around the despondent boy, but he is too preoccupied with the darkness to notice. At his side are eight wands attached to steps that ascend into the morning sunlight. The boy could easily follow these rails to freedom, but he disregards their usefulness because they are broken. A ninth wand burns like a torch from behind. Its glowing flame symbolizes the rekindling of the boy's spirit and reminds him not to quit. The fire warms his downcast spirit while giving him the power to see his predicament in an entirely new light.

Upright meanings:

The Nine of Wands encourages you to summon your inner strength and use it to find your way out of a complicated situation. Although success may seem out of reach, take heart knowing that you are extremely close to achieving all that you have struggled for. Keep climbing higher and maintain your momentum! Do not be afraid to step up to the challenges that lie ahead.

The Nine of Wands recommends that you expand your awareness in order to recognize nearby opportunities. You must also be willing to learn from your mistakes. Do not let your setbacks get you down. Hold your head up and remember that failure always marks the path to success.

In addition, the card may be a metaphor for the difficulties one might experience when trying to acquire a new set of skills. Perhaps you are finding it hard to make progress because you have hit a plateau during your quest for mastery. When things get tough, you must keep your determination blazing so that you can attain the breakthrough you desire.

"Flying Free at Last", sketch (2007)

The boy was unable to spread his wings within the confines of the dreary labyrinth. This could mean that talent alone will not be enough to take him to the top.

When reversed, the Nine of Wands could mean that you have reached the point of physical, mental or emotional burnout. Repeated disappointments have snuffed the passionate fire that once raged deep inside of you. As darkness suffocates your motivation and overwhelms your willpower, it may seem impossible to pick yourself up and carry on. In this demoralized state, you may finally decide to give up on your dreams, believing they are beyond reach or no longer worth pursuing.

My son was reluctant to model his feet for the card, however, he changed his mind quickly once I promised him some new art supplies.

Eight of Wands

A peasant woman prepares to rid her land of seven wands growing in the field. She believes that if she fails to move quickly, the cluster will multiply and overrun the land. The intrusive wands stand defiantly against the will of the peasant. Each bears a clean cut mark on top; evidence that someone once attempted to hack them down in the past, but was unable to stop them from growing back again. The determined peasant fixes her gaze on the stubborn wands, vowing to do everything in her power to put a permanent end to this nuisance. An eighth wand serves as a scythe as she readies to cut them all down with a single stroke.

A black crow flies swiftly into the scene carrying a handwritten letter in its beak. This might be an omen warning the peasant not to be impulsive, for the action she is about to take will have unforeseen and irreversible consequences. Although the wands disgust and enrage the peasant's sensibilities, they may be providing her with an undiscovered benefit. The letter will likely affect the outcome of this situation if she receives it before swinging her mighty blade.

Upright meanings:

The Eight of Wands illustrates a moment in your life when you may be acting in haste. This could be because you are anxious to get started on a project, or wish to get something unpleasant over with as quickly as possible. Regardless of your situation, you may want to stop and reconsider your current course of action. Do not do something you might regret. Be sure to get all the facts before making an important decision.

In this card, the wheat field could represent one's fertile mind. The wands may then symbolize unwelcome thoughts or emotions that keep popping up despite attempts to wipe them out. Do not despair! New insights will come to change your perception of this growing problem for the better.

The Eight of Wands might also signify the urgency to eliminate bad habits. It is time to be strong and take control of your life. Do not hesitate or let anything prevent you from slashing your negative behaviors down to size!

Finally, the Eight of Wands could be a symbolic expression of hate and anger. Beware! This woman's formidable energy is poised to destroy something out of spite, jealousy or envy.

Reversed meanings:

In a reversed position, the Eight of Wands represents a period of stagnation in your work. Outside distractions prevent or delay you from completing your tasks. Despite the frustration, it is crucial for you to concentrate on the job at hand. If you truly want to realize your dreams, you must keep your mind focused and ignore all interruptions.

VIII

*"Eight of Wands",
rough sketch (2007)*

Additionally, you may be unconsciously sabotaging your own efforts. Besides an external influence, the black crow in this card could also symbolize an internal hindrance such as procrastination, resistance, or self-doubt. Now is the perfect time to look within and strike down any character trait that stops you from taking action on your plans. Do not wait any longer!

"Swampy Grassland" background photo taken at Heckscher Park, Long Island, New York

"Medieval Peasant Plowing the Field", ink sketch (2007)

Seven of Wands

A bewildered child emerges from the thicket after being lost inside for several days. Against overwhelming odds, she has finally discovered a path that will lead her home and into the arms of her grateful mother. The fiery blooms of seven wands glow like torches in the night, marking the end of her harrowing ordeal.

While she was astray in the darkness, the child courageously fought back against her fears instead of cowering in the shadows. Night after night, she desperately searched for the exit only to wander around in circles. The coarse weeds and knotted roots on the ground gave her bare feet nasty blisters, but she never stopped to rest. She relentlessly plowed through the bramble, ignoring the sharp thorns that tore her dress and sliced her skin. Refusing to become a victim of her terrible surroundings, the determined child kept moving forward until she eventually broke free from her nightmare.

Upright meanings:

The Seven of Wands is an assuring sign that a traumatic experience will most likely lead to a personal breakthrough. At this moment, life is putting you to the test. Realize that your pain and suffering serve to strengthen your character. This is the time to push your mind and body to extremes. By doing so, you will bring out abilities you never knew you had. Stay resourceful as you persistently pursue your objective. Remember, you are not just *going* through this hardship, but *growing* through it, as well! Take comfort in knowing you will come out of this difficult situation a better person than before.

The Seven of Wands may also predict a victorious win over intense competition. Realize that success will not be easy. Your challengers will come at you from every angle and try to thwart your ambitions. Know that you will triumph if you put up the fight of your life!

Additionally, the Seven of Wands could signify someone fleeing a hostile environment. This person's survival depends on taking responsibility for his or her own rescue and getting out of danger. The card might also mean that you will successfully escape mental confusion. Because of your tenacity, thorny problems will begin to make sense, and hidden solutions will become apparent.

Reversed meanings:

When reversed, the Seven of Wands usually indicates an ongoing state of uncertainty and confusion. Self-doubt obscures the route to your success. Unfortunately, you may have tricked yourself into believing that there is no possible way out of a complicated situation. Do not lose faith in your own abilities. Know that you will ultimately find your direction in life if you keep on looking and never give up.

"Hunted by the Beasts in the Thicket"

"Boldly Confronting the Salivating Monsters"

The initial idea I had for the Seven of Wands pictured the little girl fending off a pack
of wild beasts.

During her tribulation through the swampy mist, the girl came across the rotted skeletons of other lost children lying in the mud. They silently beckoned her to give up her struggle and sleep with them in the quagmire forever.

My daughter was always willing to lend a helping hand when it came to modeling for the deck.

Six of Wands

Tonight, there is a celebration in the woods. The grand metamorphosis has finally occurred! A new being emerges victoriously from a moonlit flower bud, the likes of which no one has ever before seen. Five devotees marvel in awe and hold their wands high in honor of the event. With a flowering sixth wand, the extraordinary creature bestows good fortune on all souls present.

The remarkable creature rises with a set of beautifully formed insect wings. With this enhancement, she can fly to new heights and reach destinations once thought unachievable. During her transformation, she acquired many other unique characteristics. For example, while most citizens in the Deviant Moon Tarot have a blue-sided face to represent their subconscious mind, hers has become red. This variation shows her enlightened shift in consciousness, and that she no longer thinks like everyone else. In addition to her ears, she now has a variety of insect antennae growing on her head, which amplify her intuitive awareness and receptivity.

The creature's multiple hands signify that she has gained the skill and dexterity to turn her imagination into reality. Some of her hands face up to receive grace from the heavens, while others grip the wood of her earthly wand. This suggests that she trusts in higher powers, yet maintains control over her own destiny.

The leafy crown worn by the creature represents the concept of immortality or resurrection. New life rises from old in a perpetual state of change. An inverted amber teardrop dangles from the center of the crown. This powerful gemstone helps to turn negative thoughts into positive energy.

Emblazoned on the creature's stellar dress is a golden sun. It peeks out from underneath her black collar and dominates the small crescent moon below. This relationship symbolizes the end of night and the dawn of a bright new era.

Upright meanings:

The Six of Wands illustrates the glorious results of education and personal development. You will reap great rewards once you enlighten your mind and modify your old philosophies. Through disciplined effort, you will learn valuable skills that can advance your station in life. Expect to have a breakthrough or revelation so profound that you can never go back to being the way you were before. Others will admire your success story and consider your drastic transformation as nothing short of a miracle!

The triumphant Six of Wands might also represent the ascent of a hero, a celebrity, or someone of noteworthy status. Many will idolize this person's legendary deeds. Through hard work and dedication, you, too, might attain widespread fame and finally get the credit

"The Levitating Creature", ink study (2007)

you deserve! As your popularity soars, you must remember to remain grateful to your loyal supporters. Be sure to acknowledge them more than they acknowledge you.

Reversed meanings:

In a reversed position, the Six of Wands says that you may not achieve the level of success you desire. Perhaps you failed to develop the skills necessary to be outstanding in your field. In order to make progress, you must go back and improve yourself further.

Maybe you accomplished something incredible but received little recognition. Although you might be feeling proud and excited over your triumph, no one else seems to care. What's more, you may have reached a high status only to find that your followers have lost their respect for you. Without their support, your exalted prestige will surely collapse.

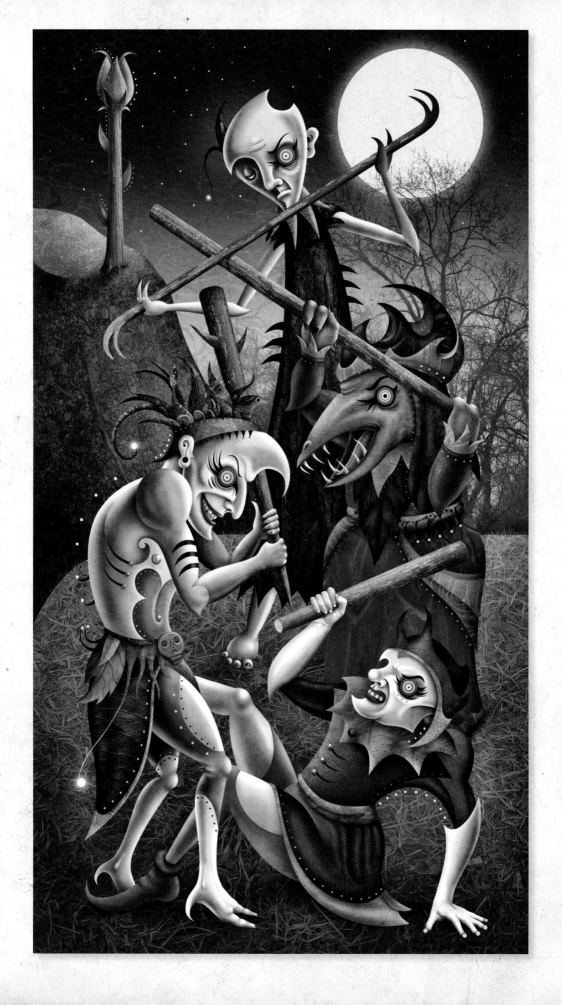

FIVE OF WANDS

A violent conflict has broken out in the forest! Citizens from various factions are at war over a solitary wand blooming on a hill, the last of its kind. Behaving like wild animals, they resort to a vicious battle of wands to achieve superiority. Each fighter knows that if he obtains the precious plant, his people will be in control of its seeds and will gain the power to starve out rival clans. High above the mayhem, the full moon warps all common sense as the combatants spiral into frenzied madness.

Hatred and prejudice are the underlying motives for this inane display of aggression. In truth, these warring citizens are using the flowering wand as an excuse to brutalize and kill one another. Chances are that they, along with the flower, will soon become extinct.

Luckily, the belligerents can easily put a stop to this self-made crisis whenever they choose. If they decide to forsake their ignorance and cooperate with one another, their clans could share the flower seeds and grow prosperous new gardens in their respective dominions.

Upright meanings:

The Five of Wands represents a period of disharmony and friction between groups of people. Rational thought will give way to insanity as opposing forces struggle to come out on top. Legal disputes, a hostile clash with neighbors, or fights over scarce resources are all some of the ways to interpret this unruly card. In severe cases, it might foretell of anarchy, rioting in the streets, or mutiny against authority. Furthermore, the Five of Wands could signify racism or xenophobia.

This card may also refer to a fierce competition or a sporting event in which ruthless players do anything necessary to win a valued prize, even if it means harming an opponent. It can also denote a situation where individuals vie for the attention of someone of the opposite sex.

Besides an external struggle, the Five of Wands could symbolize an internal conflict, as well. Contradictory needs and desires are pulling your emotions apart. In this chaotic state of mind, you will find it hard to make decisions or choose among alternatives.

Reversed meanings:

Get a hold of yourself and stop bickering! Realize that the senseless battle you are waging against your rivals must end. It is time to put all differences aside and peacefully negotiate with one another to solve a problem. Although it may be hard to agree on all points, each needs to respect the other's opinion. Know there is hidden strength in your diversity.

In addition, the reversed card could be warning you to avoid conflict at all costs. Mind your own business and stay out of trouble. Do not get caught up in everyone else's lunacy.

Individual studies for the combatants (2007)
The guardian of the last blooming flower

An intruding settler defends against a crazed savage.

A mercenary warrior prepares for attack.

The hostile citizens use dry, dead wands in their fight for dominance. These dehydrated sticks represent their dying societies. The combatants seek not only to take the seeds from the last succulent wand, but also to sap the life force running through it, hoping the green energy will rejuvenate their withered kingdoms.

Four of Wands

Abride and groom walk hand-in-hand up the path leading to their new home. The house resembles a giant flower bulb that is ready to grow into an enormous plant with many blooming branches. Four massive wands serve to stabilize the structure while providing a strong base on which the newlyweds can build their lives together.

Ivy vines bind the newlyweds' clasped hands, a symbol of wedlock and mutual commitment. As they gaze directly into each other's eyes, they convey the loving connection between their souls and show that they see themselves as trusted equals.

A full moon hovers above the scene glowing with satisfaction. Its silvery light illuminates a delicate spider web leading up to the front door of the couple's dwelling. Using the web as a ladder, the newlyweds will soon climb into an intimate world of joy and tranquility.

Upright meanings:

The Four of Wands stands for a long lasting partnership set up on a firm foundation. This might be in reference to one's marriage, and it could extend into domestic life. Kindness, honesty, loyalty and affection are just some of the qualities needed to form sturdy pillars of support. In a caring environment like this, family members feel secure knowing they can depend on one another. Remember, turbulence will inevitably arise in any relationship, but with a durable framework you and your loved ones will be able to weather any household storm.

This card may also mean that you will soon find and move into the house of your dreams. Know that this will be an idyllic place to begin raising a family. Your family will cherish this pleasant abode, not because of the building itself, but because of the love, happiness and memorable times they will share inside.

Reversed meanings:

When the Four of Wands appears upside down, it often symbolizes domestic upheaval. Home is no longer a sanctuary. Hostility, deceit and mistrust undermine the structure of the family. Unstable household relations teeter on the verge of collapse. It might be wise to sever your ties and get out while you can before everything comes crashing down!

In this position, the card could also represent a bitter divorce. The couple involved has lost their respect for each other and they constantly disagree. There may be no chance of saving this unstable marriage because it was never built on solid ground from the beginning.

An early design for the pod house with thatched roofing (2007)

If you examine this card closely, you may notice that the crescents of the newlyweds' heads form the top half of a heart. This is symbolic of the love they share. However, even as they join hands and hearts, their heads do not quite touch, since the two remain independent and individual in their thinking.

THREE OF WANDS

Upon a grassy hill, an expectant mother anxiously awaits the blooming of three wands. A chunk of orange amber glows hot on her belt, signaling that birth is imminent. Having committed massive energy into the growth of this new life, she reflects on the journey that has brought her to this moment. Although she is hopeful for success, the number three represents unpredictability and the chance that things may not develop as imagined.

A vine-like umbilical cord connects the young mother's swollen belly to the wands. Her warm blood streams through this vital link, which nourishes the blooms and keeps them alive. Her exposed breast shows her readiness to foster the plants after they flower; however, she keeps her other breast tucked under her arm in a guarded fashion. This might imply that she has mixed feelings about the perpetual responsibilities that lie ahead.

In the days before raising these wands from seed, the young mother was immature and wild. Nurturing something greater than herself taught her to focus on creation instead of destruction. She has flipped her fierce warrior mask around to the back like a cloak, revealing the caring side of her personality.

From afar, the deviant moon imparts its spirit upon the buds with its silver breath. The young mother has done her part, and now the universe will complete this unique creation.

Upright meanings:

The Three of Wands represents the circulation of creativity from one form to another. Like a mother with child, your life force flows into your creations and sustains them until they can survive on their own. You have given so much to bring your ideas into existence, and they are flourishing brilliantly. Although this should be an exciting time for you, vicious thoughts of self-doubt run in the back of your mind. As you contemplate your efforts, you may be wondering if you planned well enough to ensure favorable results. Stop worrying and let your remarkable conceptions unfold naturally.

Reversed meanings:

Upside down, the Three of Wands says that a creative endeavor may go wrong despite your best attempts. While you meant well and tried to think of everything, the little mistakes you made along the way could compound into a tremendous failure. Despite the disappointment, you must remember that you did not waste your time. Learn from your errors, conceive a better plan, and try again!

Perhaps the negative aspects of your character are getting the best of you, making it hard to concentrate on projects or see them to fruition. Realize that neglect or a lack of dedication may also lead to your creative shortcomings.

In this early variation, three impaled skulls mark the boundary between a pristine environment and a polluted industrial zone. Deadly toxins leached from the factories contaminate the water and encroach upon the countryside. A revised version of this abandoned design may find its way into a future deck.

Two of Wands

Spring has arrived early, and the farmer has begun planting in the fields. He is eager to get a head start on his crops; however, the harsh winter left the ground hard and dry. One after another, the farmer's tools bend and break as he uses them to dig into the hardened soil. His workmates urge him to give up and go home, believing it practical to wait until the rain comes to soften the land. But the farmer knows he has the potential to succeed despite unfavorable circumstances.

The farmer stops for a moment and sits down next to his splintered tools to ponder. As his mind scans the debris for answers, he notices two broken shovels lying by the wayside that intrigue his imagination. He pulls the wooden handles out of the dust and combines them to create a powerful new device. By channeling dual energies into a single force, he digs the first hole with ease and goes on to sow what will become a bountiful harvest.

Upright meanings:

The Two of Wands advises you that in order to achieve success, you must pool your resources together and focus your creative muscle on a specific objective. Work hard and be inventive! Integrate your mental ability with your physical strength, and then apply yourself fully to your task. Know that the effort you exert today will bring multiple rewards tomorrow.

The Two of Wands symbolizes the unification of forces. This could mean that you need to form a partnership to attain a common goal. You will gain tremendous personal growth once you ally yourself with someone of similar talents and ambitions.

This card may also imply the need to restructure an organization to make it more effective. Streamline your business and concentrate only on the most productive activities.

Reversed meanings:

When upturned, the Two of Wands denotes your inability to think creatively. This may be happening because you are dividing your attention among too many things. During this time, you will experience difficulty composing your thoughts into workable solutions.

In a work environment, the reversed card might suggest that employees will fail to collaborate with each other, thereby botching a critical assignment.

Additionally, you might be doing something in a way that continually yields poor results, expecting eventual success. Stop driving yourself crazy and try a different method! By changing your technique and using your resources uniquely, you will finally get the elusive results you desire.

In a preliminary design, a dandy fellow strolls through a flower garden holding a blossoming wand over his shoulder. Believing his flower to be one of a kind, the sight of its twin growing on a hill surprises him. A woman's arm emerges from the man's belly and reaches out to pluck the matching flower from its roots.

Although I did not use this design, I cannibalized parts of it for use in other cards. The woman's arm found its way into the Six of Pentacles, and several tribesmen wound up fighting over the wand on the hill in the Five of Wands.

ACE OF WANDS

The willowy angel heralds all that is good as she cradles new life in her arms. Wrapped in a peapod, her infant rests peacefully while building energy for the day ahead. As morning approaches, the child's innocent face tears though the husk while his consciousness slowly awakens to the world around him.

The angel carries a massive torch in her third hand. She will use it to ignite lethargic minds and spread passionate creativity. The angel has pruned the branches, showing that she is willing to forgo anything she considers unnecessary for the benefit of the whole. A large beetle crawls up the torch and comes dangerously close to the roaring flame. The insect is typical of the fierce qualities one must have in order to pursue a burning desire. This beetle can also represent resurrection, rebirth or spontaneity.

The angel wears a crown of succulent ivy leaves, a festive sign of prosperity. It might also represent a virtuous marriage. The large amber diamond in the center of the wreath signifies the angel's intelligence. The bunch of golden grapes that hang along the sides represents her fertility, as well as the personal sacrifices she has made in life.

The angel's organic hair consists of long green vines and autumn leaves. Trees blooming with radiant orbs grow on top of her head, forming a lively forest that illuminates the darkness.

A graceful pair of moth wings flutters on the angel's back, giving her the ability to fly across the heavens. Like a moth, she regularly navigates by moonlight and courageously follows the light of her intuitive spirit. The beautiful wings also suggest her transition from one stage of life to another.

Upright meanings:

Let the Ace of Wands be your muse, for she will give you an unprecedented surge of creative inspiration. With her guidance, bold new ideas will grow from your mind and branch out in every direction possible. Be sure to take action on them now while your enthusiasm is high. Like a blazing fire, it will be difficult to contain your red-hot thoughts. Do not be surprised if it gets hectic managing the many blessings of your fertile imagination.

In a reading, the Ace of Wands could also symbolize birth or the start of a daring new venture. These are exciting times, filled with hope and promise. Know that the seeds you plant today are destined to mature into a robust entity.

Lastly, the card might stand for one's personal transformation or reinvention. Get set for a new and better life to emerge from the old.

Reversed meanings:

When reversed, the Ace of Wands represents a period of low mental, physical or spiritual energy. In this dampened state, life will seem subdued and unrewarding. You will not have

"A Maiden with all Four Seasons in Her Hair, and a Cocooned Infant", early studies (2007)

the strength or desire to pursue your creative ideas. Know that you will never realize your dreams until you revive your fiery passion. Look deep within and you will find powerful reasons to be inspired once again.

In this position, the card could also mean that you are spreading your creative energy too thin. Although thrilling at first, the multiple projects you have taken on are becoming too much to handle. Consequently, you might have lost your motivation to work on anything. It is time to put everything down and focus your talents exclusively on a single idea.

The card pictures the angel with three hands. This shows that she has the capacity to assume numerous responsibilities while still maintaining her creative aspirations.

Medieval paintings of the Madonna and Child
influenced the design of the Ace of Wands.

"The Muse with her Newborn Pupa", preliminary sketch (2007)

Suit of Cups

The Realm of Cups contains the joys of life, as well as the sorrows. The kindhearted residents here are essentially optimistic, and they strive to build harmonious relationships with their fellow citizens. By expressing their innermost feelings to one another, they gain valuable insight into their own souls. Although they rely on keen intuition for guidance, they sometimes allow the tides of emotion to dictate their actions. Once these impassioned people learn to manage their moods in a positive way, they will undoubtedly lead lives of abundant success and fulfillment.

King of Cups

The insightful King of Cups stands proudly on a sand dune by the sea. Raising his jeweled goblet, he toasts the citizens of his coastal kingdom, wishing them all long-lasting joy and prosperity. With gentle compassion, his mind reflects on the liquid held inside the cup, signifying the attentive consideration he gives to the emotional wellness of his people.

The King is a flamboyant character whose soul overflows with artistic style and flair. He wears regal attire made of fish and octopus skins, which he skillfully designed and created himself. His bare foot protrudes from under his gold-trimmed robe, ready to step across the beach. He refuses to let etiquette stifle his free-roaming spirit. The loose way in which the King holds his military fork is also suggestive of his easy-going personality. Being a kindhearted leader, he prefers to befriend his royal subjects rather than forcefully impose his will on them.

Behind the King, a full moon lights the sky with luminous intuition. Its silvery beams gently kiss the surface of the ocean while stirring the mysterious depths below with sparkling energy. Celestial blessings also appear as a brilliant star that shines from the heavens and reassures its earthly counterpart below. This miraculous occurrence demonstrates the relationship between the spiritual and material realms, which the King wisely uses to help lead his followers into a life of self-realization.

On the horizon, a trading vessel glides across the tranquil water, delivering the King's message of peace and goodwill to foreign lands. When it returns home, the ship will import

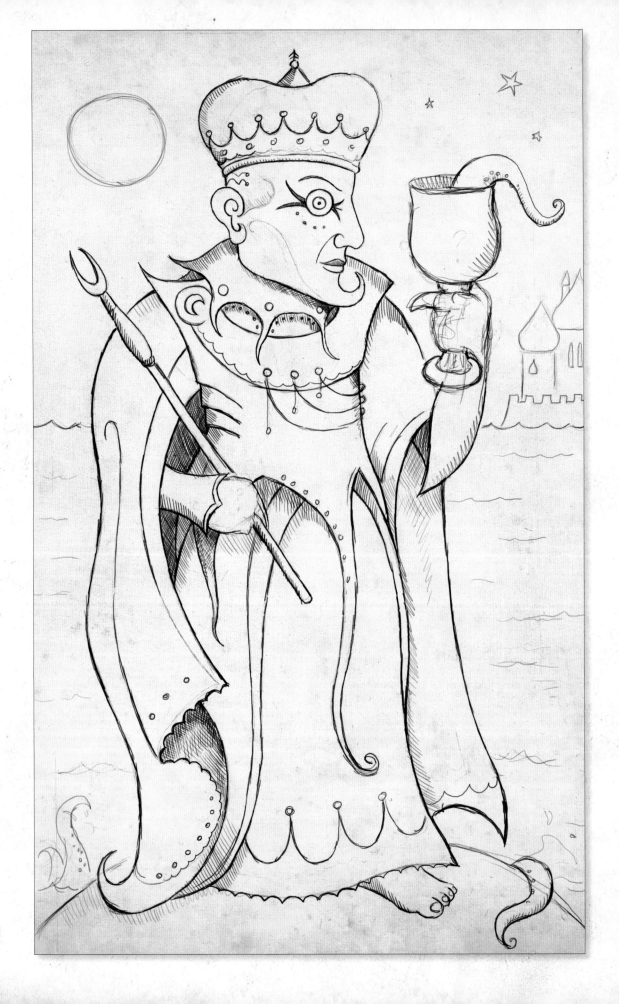

all of the exotic customs and traditions it has encountered on its travels. Because he enriches the citizens with cultural diversity, the King strengthens the fabric of his entire dominion.

Upright meanings:

The King of Cups is in full command of his emotional state. Let him be your mentor as you learn to control your innermost feelings. Know that by maintaining your composure during a time of crisis, you will be better able to solve any problem. In addition, someone may be looking to you for advice or counsel. Be sympathetic to the needs of others without seeking a reward in return. Become an ambassador of harmony and bring out the good in everyone you meet. The caring example you set will be an inspiration to all.

The broad-minded King also recommends that you let your creativity reign. Do not be afraid to embrace your eccentricities. Unleash the wondrous beauty inside of you, and turn whatever you touch into a magnificent work of art.

Reversed meanings:

When reversed, emotions spill like water out of the King's overturned cup. This could mean that you will have a difficult time dealing with someone who is emotionally unstable, or who is prone to melodramatic outbursts. Be mindful that such a temperamental character only seeks to manipulate you with their turbulent moods! Then again, perhaps you are the one having trouble containing your emotions. Mental upset drains the very essence of your life. Imagination and creativity seem depleted. Now is the time to refocus your thoughts and take control of these overwhelming feelings before they lead you to ruin.

As always, the court cards set the color palette for the entire suit. Cool colors such as blue, aqua and purple were chosen to illustrate the calm demeanor of this watery realm. Splashes of red were added for contrast, which intensified some of the heartfelt emotions of the citizens.

The ornate cups held by the royal family were made by manipulating a photo of a thin copper pipe. The common cups seen throughout the suit came from a single gold chalice found in a yard sale.

King of Cups, rough sketch (2006), left

QUEEN OF CUPS

The benevolent Queen of Cups makes her way along the shoreline holding her glorious chalice with care. With this vessel, she delivers a drink of compassion to quench the emotional thirst of all her people. Her open hand extends with kindness, ready to catch a drop of water that has spilled over the brim. This loving deed demonstrates her thoughtful nature and shows that she will always reach out to help those in need.

A crescent moon illuminates the Queen's unconscious mind as it silently hangs over her shoulder. Its silvery light clarifies her intuition and intensifies the flow of her psychic abilities. Her sensitivity spreads from her head down to her feet, where she feels every grain of sand between her toes as she steps across the beach. Although the Queen travels wherever her heart leads her, we see her facing to the left. This could mean that she is so busy looking to console others that she sometimes loses sight of herself.

In the distance, a lighthouse serves as a guiding beacon over dark seas. Like the Queen, it directs souls who have gone adrift into the safety of a sheltered harbor. A large sailing ship ignores the calling and chooses to head out in the opposite direction. The Queen would do well to learn from this example and realize that she cannot always save everyone she meets.

UPRIGHT MEANINGS:

The Queen of Cups personifies a tenderhearted soul who will enter your life to soothe the pain of your emotional wounds. This caring person sympathizes with your worries and will wipe the tears away from your crying eyes. Like a devoted mother concerned for her children, she will be there to show you the way during uncertain times. She will patiently listen to your problems and offer comforting advice.

The gentle Queen may also be asking you to follow in her noble footsteps. Be selfless in your actions and find ways to contribute to the greater good. Make it your mission to replenish the shriveled spirit of someone in desperate need with unconditional love and acceptance.

REVERSED MEANINGS:

When reversed, the Queen of Cups represents an emotionally insecure person who saps the energy of all those around her. This pathetic character demands endless reassurance and will manipulate your feelings without remorse. Because she is the taker in a relationship, she will bleed your poor heart dry. Unfortunately, nothing you give will ever satisfy the thirsty needs of someone like this.

In this overturned position, the queen's chalice could signify someone who is emotionally drained. This worn out person has given so much to others that she has nothing left inside for herself. She used to be so affectionate, but now seems irritable or depressed. Know that showing her the same compassion she used to give you will help turn her cup upright again.

The reversed Queen might also assume the role of an unfit mother or caretaker. This insensitive guardian offers no love to her neglected children, and may eventually abandon all who depend on her.

The regal gemstones that adorn the Queen (as well as many other deviant characters) are actually photos of little glass beads taken from my daughter's jewelry-making kit.

The misguided ship seen in the background of this card appears two other times in the deck. It can be found on the World card, where it returns home after a triumphant journey, as well as on the Death card, where its ruined hull sinks beneath the waves of a poisoned sea.

Queen of Cups, rough sketch (2006), left

KNIGHT OF CUPS

The Knight of Cups presents his remarkable find to the world, fulfilling the mission set forth by the King. For eons, he has been searching beneath the boundless sea, determined to retrieve this mythical treasure. Although it has been immersed for so long in saltwater, this prized chalice is in pristine condition. Forged by spiritual energy, the metal is impervious to the corrosion of earthly elements and will last far into eternity.

Unlike most warriors, the Knight of Cups bears no weapons of war. He is a romantic lover of life, and he uses both hands to support his magnificent gift instead of waging battle. Although he is peaceful, the Knight also tends to be overemotional and defensive at times. Like the conch shells littering the shore around him, he has created a suit of armor to protect his sensitive soul and shield his feelings from outside negativity.

The Knight's suit of armor was a heavy burden during his expedition. Its weight not only slowed him from attaining his souvenir, but it almost pulled him down permanently to the ocean floor. Once polished to a lustrous copper sheen, it is now weathered and green with patina. The bottom half of the suit has broken away, caused by the mutation of the Knight's legs into a swirling eel-like tail. This tail shows that he is gradually becoming adept at navigating his aquatic environment, which will, in turn, allow him to accomplish future tasks with greater ease.

UPRIGHT MEANINGS:

Dive down into the depths of your subconscious and extract an intangible idea. Although the answer you are looking for might come in a dream, it is up to you to manifest it into reality. Like the indomitable Knight, you also have the power to fulfill your ambitions by taking smart and persistent action. Be relentless in your pursuit of victory and be willing to make great sacrifices to achieve your desires.

Good news is headed your way! The Knight of Cups might arrive in a reading as a messenger offering an unexpected opportunity. This could come as a curious invitation or proposition, which could lead to joy and satisfaction if accepted.

Reversed meanings:

When the Knight of Cups makes a reversed appearance, he brings bad tidings to your virtuous ambitions. Be forewarned that the greatness you seek might end in a disappointing letdown. Alluring opportunities may surface, but they will only yield frustration and regret. Understand that if you truly want success in your life, you will have to develop new skills and shed unfavorable aspects of your personality.

The Most Valuable Treasures

One of my favorite things to do with my family is walk along the beaches of Long Island hunting for unique stones and seashells. To me, it seems as if these marine artifacts somehow absorb and contain the happy memories of the day. The shells pictured in this card came from a well-spent afternoon with my daughter discovering the seaside world together.

Knight of Cups, rough sketch (2006), left

PAGE OF CUPS

The young Page of Cups has been wandering beside the coast, daydreaming in fantasy while filling her chalice with water from the sea. Her childhood days are fading fast, and new responsibilities loom on the horizon. Although nature calls her to become a woman, deep down inside she aspires to be a fish. Disguised as a sea creature, she tries to avoid what seems inevitable by assuming the identity she desires. To become a real fish, however, the Page must boldly venture out into the ocean and evolve through adversity.

The Page is filled with raw imagination and fledgling desires. Intense thoughts turn into reality as a small fish suddenly bursts out of her chalice and looks her right in the eye. Instead of being frightened by this oddity, the Page naturally reacts with childlike delight and playfully tickles the fish under the chin. As their spirits connect, the fish shows the page the value of her ideas by producing a glowing pearl on the tip of its tongue. Along with this precious gift, the fish imparts its wisdom, advising the Page to live life on her own terms and courageously manifest her own destiny.

In the background, two possible outcomes await the Page. On the left, a barren island represents what she can expect if she does not strive to be all that her heart calls her to be. To the right, the gigantic tail of a whale gives the Page a glimpse of the greatness lying beneath should she decide to take the risk and pursue her dreams.

Upright meanings:

The lively Page of Cups personifies the enthusiastic energy needed to take you to a higher form of existence. Lose all inhibitions and design your life with outrageous creativity. Be confident in your individuality as you progress into the future. Newly planted beliefs are coming of age and are ready to grow into mature philosophies. Remember the importance of staying young at heart as your logical mind expands its awareness. However, do not be juvenile in your thinking if you truly wish to fulfill your ambitions.

Take heed of your intuition! Listen to the whispers of your unconscious mind, for it is trying to communicate to you through abstract or symbolic references. Inspired ideas will abruptly materialize from unexpected sources and bring you priceless rewards, provided you give them the attention they deserve. Take the time to look deep within yourself in order to decipher their secret meanings.

Reversed meanings:

When dealt in reverse, the Page of Cups might signify someone with stunted emotional growth. This immature brat has a hard time controlling her overblown feelings, and will likely throw a fit if things do not go her way. Her lack of imagination and vision cripples her potential. A small-minded person like this fears going out and discovering all the wondrous

possibilities the world has to offer. Instead, she would rather stay where she is and depend on others for simple things she could easily manage for herself.

In this flipped position, the card could also be a sign of frustrated creativity. You might find that your ingenious imagination is not flowing as freely as normal. Know that inspiration is always all around you, but you may have to explore unusual sources to uncover it.

Another aspect of this reversed card could tell of bizarre or frightful ideas that pop into your mind without warning. Although these upsetting thoughts might be difficult to face, you must not ignore the important message they are trying to convey!

Drawing in sketchbook, 1984 (Age 17)

The fish suit worn by the Page of Cups was inspired by an old doodle in my teenage sketchbook. This sketch pictured a mother and father giving their difficult child some necessary parental advice. Coincidentally, part of the meaning behind the reversed Page of Cups card fits perfectly with the concept of this little drawing.

Page of Cups, rough sketch (2006), left

TEN OF CUPS

A wounded soldier returning from war is embraced by his loving family. At last, they are all united again after what seemed to be an eternity of longing and separation. The happiness they share on this magnificent night transcends the heavens, causing the stars to sparkle with intense delight, and the moon to swell to its fullest capacity. Ten golden cups rise overhead in celebration of this joyful reunion.

The road home was not easy for the weary soldier to travel. He survived by keeping a strong vision of his family foremost in his mind, and he did whatever it took to get back to them. A wheel serving as an artificial limb replaces his lower leg lost in combat. This shows that he has found a way to keep moving on through life, despite the intensity of his hardships. In the background, the curved horizon represents the many miles journeyed across the globe. Peacefully docked on the left is his warship, while on the right, his home welcomes him with its doors wide open, revealing the glowing warmth that waits inside.

The soldier may have a difficult time fitting back into domestic life after his harrowing experience. The war may have ended, but a mental battle still rages in his mind. His damaged head is cracked open, and a large chunk of it is missing. A bloodstained bandage is all that keeps his entire skull from falling apart. Although she cannot fully understand his anguish, the soldier's devoted wife puts her head against his and caresses his face, showing that she empathizes with his pain and will share in his emotional burdens. Through their love for each other, they will undoubtedly find a way to heal.

All four symbols of the tarot have been brought together to balance the overall harmony of this happy scene. The infant rides his father's shoulder, gleefully waving a small golden pentacle brought back as a token from foreign lands. Twisting a wand through the air like a baton, the soldier's older son ceremoniously marches around his family and reenacts his father's heroic battles. The soldier's sword rests peacefully in its sheath, symbolizing the end of hostility and bloodshed. It remains close at hand, however, should he need to defend his homeland once more.

UPRIGHT MEANINGS:

The Ten of Cups portrays a loving and harmonious relationship among family members, or any group of like-minded people sharing a common dream. Rejoice, and revel in your mutual good fortune! Life seems to have finally reached the point of perfection after times of great sacrifice and adversity. By nurturing the needs of one another, you have all created a home base that is tranquil, content, and secure. Know that lasting happiness and satisfaction will come from your emotions, not by way of material possessions. You must also remember that you will never attain true fulfillment by chance. You and your family must be committed to working hard together for the good of the group. This card can

In this preliminary sketch, a plump infant holds up a fig leaf to symbolize his family's return to peaceful times. The drawing also pictures the soldier and his wife sharing a tender kiss.

also tell of a long-awaited reunion coming in the near future. Now is the ideal occasion to reconnect with an estranged relative or to solidify the existing bond among your kindred.

Reversed meanings:

Unfortunately, when the Ten of Cups appears in reverse, it represents upturned family relationships and domestic turmoil. Infighting between the members of your clan makes the home feel more like a battlefield than a sanctuary. Unhappiness might stem from the lack of respect, abuse or neglect of people who should be caring for one another. Instead of love and harmony, the only thing your family seems to experience is discord and dysfunction. Selfish motives undermine the very foundation of the household, making it virtually impossible to work together as a team. Additionally, you may wish to consider if the pursuit of material gain is taking precedence over the family's emotional well-being.

"Young Boy with Pentacle"

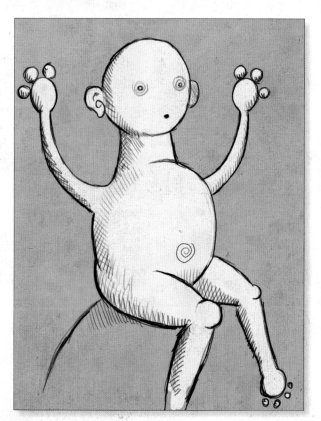

"Egg-Bodied Infant"

NINE OF CUPS

A well-dressed youth sits alone on a secluded beach, silently meditating to the rhythm of the ocean waves. Vivid daydreams sharpen his intuitive awareness, causing him to notice an old silver lamp half buried in the sand. Picking it up with excitement, he vigorously rubs off the dirt to examine his newfound discovery. Without warning, a spinning cloud of indigo smoke pours out of the spout and materializes into a magnificent genie. Grateful for his freedom, the genie folds his arms together and prepares to bestow a wish upon his new master, who wonders in amazement at the apparition he has unwittingly released.

For centuries, the genie had been held captive in darkness, unable to move in the cramped confines of the little lamp. Despite all his magical abilities, he was helpless to escape on his own. Now that the genie is loose, his restless spirit yearns to stretch out as far as possible and exercise his stifled talents. He opens his third eye to let in the light of dawn and awakens his mind to a higher plane of consciousness. As he ascends into the morning air, the genie demonstrates his power by levitating nine golden chalices in a ring of mystical energy.

The rotating vessels represent the material rewards the boy could attain by acting on his thoughts and desires until they become a reality. Before the genie passes the chalices on to the boy, he warns him that they will not guarantee his happiness. Regardless of their value, the vessels will remain empty if the boy takes them at the expense of his personal fulfillment.

UPRIGHT MEANINGS:

Discover and let loose the pent up forces inside you! Realize that you have the innate ability to obtain anything you wish for by summoning your infinite potential and putting it to practice. Open your mind with childlike curiosity and expand your way of thinking. The universe is more than willing to serve your demands; however, the divine gifts you want must be worked for and earned. Nothing worthy will come to you without effort or sacrifice. Know that the actions you take today will manifest into the satisfying future you desire.

In order to arouse your creative genius, you must remove yourself from the distractions of daily life and listen to the soft voice of your imagination. The inspiration you seek will flow freely once you immerse your mind in absolute silence. Visualize your dreams and focus your thoughts on a clear image of your desires. By patiently doing this, you will begin the process of attracting all that you long for into your life.

Reversed meanings:

When the Nine of Cups appears in reverse, it means that you might be sitting around wishing for your dreams to come true without taking action on your own. Your extraordinary potential remains bottled up inside, where it withers away and weakens with every day that passes.

In the end, you may get exactly what you wish for, but might soon discover it is not all you imagined or hoped it would be. Although success is yours, your heart remains dissatisfied.

Arabesque buildings originally appeared in the background of the card, but were omitted to emphasize the tranquil and uncluttered surroundings needed to release one's creative potential.

Rough sketch (2006), left

Eight of Cups

The woman in red has decided to abandon her old ways, for they are no longer relevant in her life. Wanting no part of the past, she holds her hands up in disgust and separates herself from the gloom. Empowering thoughts cause the ends of her hair to spark with excitement as she looks to move on to brighter situations.

The lonely cemetery that the woman escapes from represents all that is dead to her. By changing her mindset, she has come to realize that she needs to grow to stay alive; otherwise she will end up buried in the dirt, as well. Behind her, six gold cups stand neatly stacked on a grave monument. Although they seem alluring, these objects represent the detrimental habits and obsessions she once indulged in.

The delicate ribbon that once bound the woman to this lifeless setting always seemed to her like an unbreakable chain. For years, she tried to untie herself but could never figure out the complexity of the knot. By thinking about what she wanted in life instead of dwelling over what she did not want, the woman began to take forward steps away from the negativity. She leaves behind the stubborn knot, still wrapped around the base of the seventh cup.

The fleeing woman tiptoes quietly past the tombs so as not to disturb the wretched souls sleeping below. If they were to awake, these needy spirits would do all in their power to hold the woman back and pull her down into the grave. One last golden cup waits in front of her, which could mean that the temptation to return to her former behaviors will most likely follow her into the future. In order to maintain the vibrancy of her flaming red dress, the woman will need to stop her thoughts from wandering and keep her mind focused on the righteous path ahead.

Upright meanings:

The time has finally come for you to leave an emotionally unfulfilling situation. Simply walk away and never look back! You deserve a better life, but you must move beyond where you are now to experience it. Make a smart choice, and detach yourself from all that is undesirable. You may need to sever an unhealthy relationship, resign from a dead-end job, or run away from an unhappy home. Stay committed to the change you seek. Learn from the lessons of the past and let the wisdom you have gained guide you into a better future.

Reversed meanings:

In reverse, the Eight of Cups could mean that you are hesitant to remove yourself from dreaded circumstances. All of your dreams are dying off because you are afraid to leave the familiar and pursue the unknown. Mentally, you know that you should exit, but you are finding yourself restrained by an underlying emotional attachment. Willpower is weak, and you lack the resolve to disrupt the comfort of your bad habits. Understand that staying where you are will only result in your own ruin. Nothing will ever change for you unless you decide to change yourself.

In initial sketches, the runaway woman wore a depressing black dress. I later changed the dress to red to distinguish her from the somber background, as well as to express her bold passion and determination.

Gravestone in East Hampton, Long Island

I made the texture of the woman's dress by manipulating the wings of this 18th century gravestone. The idea of wings seemed fitting since the woman has taken flight from her bleak conditions to pursue a higher purpose.

Green-Wood Cemetery, Brooklyn, New York

The Eight of Cups is the only card in the deck that features tombstones in their entirety.

Seven of Cups

The talented artist works diligently in his studio, struggling to depict his subject onto canvas. With an intent stare, he focuses on seven gold cups arranged on the table before him, but does not sketch out exactly what he sees. Relying on his wild imagination, he interprets these objects the way he wishes them to be instead of representing them as they truly are. His split face demonstrates the duality of his subconscious and conscious minds, which act together to conceive an altered vision of reality.

The artist purposefully channels intuition from his head into his hands. Through self-discipline, he has learned to cultivate his imaginative thoughts and objectify them at will. Fueled by the desire to make each new creation better than the last, his dedication to practice leads him down the path of mastery.

The artist's studio serves as a sanctuary as well as a workplace. Here, he can hide from the distractions of the outside world and immerse his mind in an atmosphere of creative bliss. The energetic handprints of those he has inspired cover the walls, and some of his finest paintings surround him. Although the artist tends to work best in seclusion, he cannot be successful without the aid of others. His loyal assistant stands like a sturdy easel always there to support his efforts.

Upright meanings:

The Seven of Cups illustrates the concept of turning life into a masterpiece. Design your own experience, and do not conform to anyone's limited expectations. The fantastic ideas roaming around your head need an expressive outlet. Keep in mind that it will take the consistent development of your skills to transmute your daydreams into reality. Know that your imaginative thoughts have the power to reshape the entire world around you. Think abstractly, and your hidden genius will produce innovative results. By looking at mundane situations with a creative eye, you will gain profound insight over any problem you encounter.

Reversed meanings:

You may be presented with a problem that requires a literal solution. Keep your thoughts real and in the moment. Trust the evidence of your own eyes and do not be misled by fantasy. The answers you seek will become apparent once you cast all illusions aside and examine the obvious facts in front of you.

In this early variation (left), the artist sketches several strange symbols to represent his interpretation of the cups stacked behind him.

The artist has only just begun to sketch his ideas onto canvas. He will most likely reveal the finished painting in a future tarot deck.

A few of my seven-year-old art students made the handprints pictured on the studio wall. The children were more than happy to put their hands into the gooey paint and press them on to paper!

Six of Cups

In times long gone, children once gathered in the town center to enjoy spectacular shows at the puppet theater. Without a care in the world, they laughed aloud and clapped their hands enthusiastically at the captivating performances they witnessed. The star of these shows was the naive Punchinello. In each performance, he lost his innocence by accepting a pitchfork from the crafty devil. Although the children always called out to warn him of the terrible mistake he was about to make, poor Punchinello took the evil offering every time.

The puppets characterize the age-old dilemma of deciding between right and wrong. Though it might appear as if the puppets are alive and have free will, an unseen person hiding below the stage secretly manipulates their fateful actions. This mysterious being guides Punchinello's movements with his right hand while his left hand animates the evil personality of the devil. Like the puppets, each of us may be physically separate from one another; however, we all originate from a singular spiritual source.

Six golden cups, carved in wood relief, decorate the outside of the puppet booth. Each one serves as a small monument to the intangible quality of memories. Although they resemble actual objects, in reality, they are merely artificial handiwork. An engraved depiction of the full moon appears in the middle of this row of mock cups, breaking up their linear pattern. This exemplifies how the subconscious mind can interfere with and distort the accurate recollection of past events.

The puppet theater is an allegorical window into life's dramas. The blood-red curtain opens at birth; the story unfolds and inevitably leads to a climactic ending at death. Many more layers of symbolism appear in the backdrop. For example, the low-lying smoke clouds represent the mystery of Punchinello's obscure future. Behind this veil of confusion, there is a large, painted factory. This represents Punchinello's indoctrination into the workings of an institutionalized society. Once he is in the system, his pure spirit will become irreversibly corrupt.

The devil casts his sinister shadow over the factory's clock tower, making it barely visible to the viewer. This metaphor illustrates the times throughout our lives when we feel overpowered by temptation. The small crescent moon hanging near the devil's head intensifies his subliminal influence over gullible souls.

Sparkling stars adorn the fabricated sky inside the booth, giving hope to those who have little experience with the devious ways of the world. These shining points of light embody the dreams people could reach if they would only make wise decisions and look above the earthly enticements.

"The Child Magician Practicing Folly Instead of Skill" (2006)

Upright meanings:

Relive days of splendor through your childhood memories! Let your mind wander back to carefree times and recapture the playful fervor of your youth. The winds of nostalgia are blowing strong and stirring forgotten emotions. Now is the perfect time to reconnect with the people and places of your long-gone past.

The Six of Cups reminds us all to look at life with childlike wonder. Your inner child yearns to express itself and have fun. It would be a terrific idea to abandon your adult responsibilities for a while and allow yourself to be a bit rambunctious with old friends.

The past holds valuable insights into the problems of today. Although the Six of Cups represents a joyous occasion, the card may be an invitation to reexamine your childhood experience through an adult mindset. This may be in reference to an important turning point in your younger days. Through careful reflection, you might find that things were not as bad as they once seemed.

Reversed meanings:

When the Six of Cups appears in reverse, it may indicate the reluctance to let go of the past. Unresolved problems from long ago turn your attention backwards, making it difficult to move forward through life. In this upturned position, the card might also signify emotional pain stemming from a traumatic childhood experience. Unpleasant memories have resurfaced, and they seek to ruin the happiness of the present day.

Realize that a pivotal choice made many years ago is responsible for the woeful situation you are in today. Regardless of any guilt or regret, you must accept the fact that there is no going back in time to erase what has already taken place. Learn from all of your experiences! Although it is impossible to change the past, you are more than capable of designing a smarter future.

The passing of the devil's pitchfork over to Punchinello could be interpreted as a rite of passage or the coming of age. It can also be symbolic of the onset of puberty or loss of virginity.

"The Child Empress Chasing the Young Fool" (2006)

The children who gleefully watch the puppet show in the Six of Cups are the youthful incarnations of the Magician, the Empress, the Fool and the Hierophant.

Green-Wood Cemetery, Brooklyn, New York.

I manipulated this photo of a mausoleum door to create the puppet booth. Its use symbolizes mortality and reminds youthful souls to cherish their earthly experiences while they can.

Mental Snapshots

When I was a small child, I was perceptive enough to realize that time was fleeting. I knew that the common things around me would be remarkably different one day in the future. I tried my best to appreciate my childhood while it was still there, and I was still in it. In order to prevent my memories from becoming a vague blur as I grew up, I invented an unusual, yet priceless ritual. When I felt emotional intensity in the events around me, I stopped whatever I was doing to snap a picture with my eye. One by one, over many years, I consciously recorded and embedded the images of life into my mind. These memories are exceptionally vivid and clear. When I think of them, I have the keen sensation that I am reliving long-vanished moments in time.

As an adult, I believe I am extremely fortunate to have never lost this connection to childhood. My mental photo albums are invaluable, and serve me now as a collection of open windows into the past. Because of these magic portals, I have been able to retrieve creative ideas that would have otherwise been lost forever, and carry them back with me into the present day. The process of mentally returning to my youth is greatly responsible for the existence of the Deviant Moon Tarot.

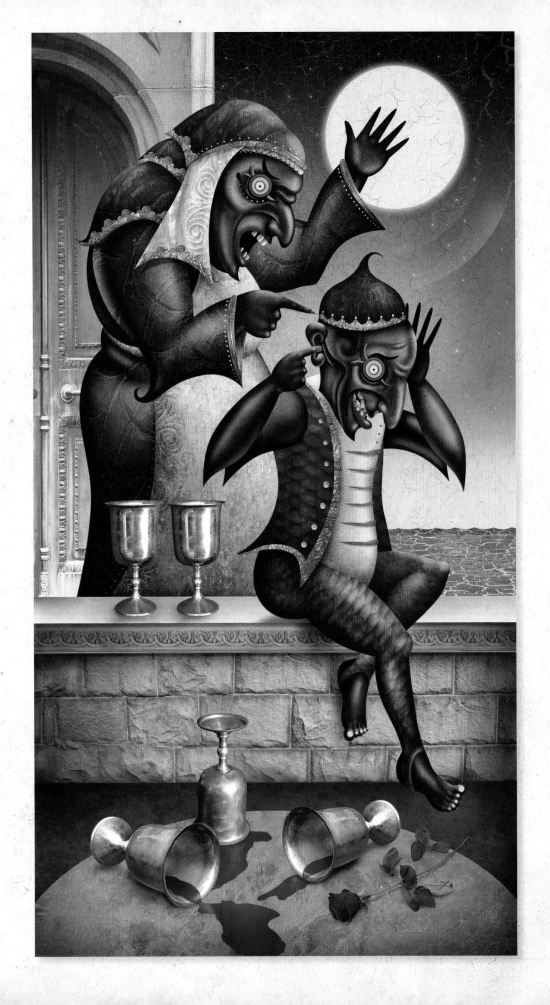

FIVE OF CUPS

A wretched shrew berates her husband over three spilled cups, the contents of which empty slowly onto the floor. Her relentless yelling shatters the tranquility of the night, as she unleashes a barrage of insults and blames him for the unfortunate loss.

The shrew blocks the full moon partially from view as she raises her hand in anger. This shows that her unyielding hostility thwarts the possibility of a satisfying relationship. As accusations fly, the nagging wife points her finger directly at her husband's head, implying his stupidity. Rather than face his wife and resolve their differences, the spineless man shuts himself off by stuffing a finger in his ear. He presses his other hand against the side of his head to keep his mind from exploding with stress.

The timid husband sits on a wall, unable to decide if he wants to stay in this poisoned relationship, or flee to the unknown on the other side. His bare foot dangles slightly above the ground reaching for a connection, but because of his short legs, his foot fails to touch the floor. This limitation is not only physical, but emotional as well, and it is suggestive of his immaturity.

The unhappy couple built the wall that separates them over the course of many years. Although the bricks seem permanent and indestructible, the wall itself is short. The couple can easily overcome this barrier once they decide to compromise with each other and show mutual respect.

In spite of their conflict, the couple has an excellent opportunity to salvage their relationship. Two cups still stand upright, for in spite of the wall that has come between husband and wife, some hope for love still remains. Amid the upset, a red rose lies in remembrance of the romance that once flourished here.

UPRIGHT MEANINGS:

The Five of Cups signifies an emotional loss resulting from a ruined relationship. Friendships have eroded and marriages are about to implode. Separation from a companion or divorce seems imminent. Although your heart yearns for love and respect of your partner, all you receive are criticism and disgust.

Be truthful with yourself and consider if you are doing all you can do to heal your damaged relationship. Though it is easy to find fault with your partner, you must realize that you have many imperfections yourself. The time has come for you to step up and take full responsibility for the mess you have made. Admit your mistakes, and do not blame anyone else for your problems. You have long ignored the warning signs, but it may not be too late to salvage the fragments of your shattered union.

This card might also refer to something in which you had high expectations, but only received disappointment. You may be experiencing regret over how miserable life has

"Peter and his Wife", colored pencil (1980)

"Keeping his Wife Very Well in a Pumpkin Shell"

turned out, and feel powerless to change anything for the better. Realize that you might be focusing on what is wrong, instead of being grateful for what is right.

Reversed meanings:

When dealt in reverse, the Five of Cups marks the definite end of a nasty relationship. The feelings you once shared with each other have run dry, and your hearts have nothing left to give. Do not let this emotional defeat leave your spirit in shambles! Although it seems hard to imagine, know that a more compatible partner waits in your near future. Remember, what failed to work in your old relationship will certainly not fare any better in a new one. If you desire your next partnership to be successful, you must be willing to learn from the past and make fundamental changes within yourself.

Peter, Peter

When I was 13 years old, I spent the summer illustrating a collection of classic nursery rhymes. For the rhyme "Peter, Peter, Pumpkin Eater", I drew a shrew wielding a rolling pin and scolding her husband. Years later, I adapted these two characters into the dysfunctional couple found in the Five of Cups.

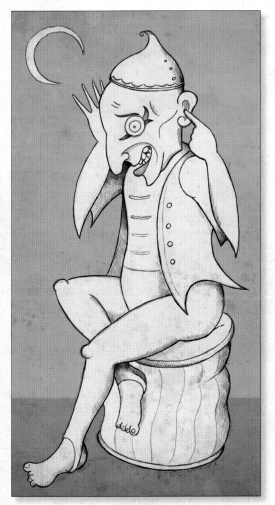

"The Browbeaten Husband and his Domineering Wife" (2006)

FOUR OF CUPS

Alone by the glow of the deviant moon, a sad woman locks herself onto a fortified balcony and quietly ponders the value of her existence. Believing she is worthless, she concludes that it is best to stay detached from the world and suffer without tears in this self-imposed exile. Boredom quickly sets in and deadens the negativity of her swollen mind. Feeling no emotion, she rests her weary chin on her hand and listlessly stares out into the vast horizon.

Several gold cups stand neatly stacked on the ledge beside the woman. Dissatisfied with life's gifts, she apathetically tosses one of the cups over the edge. Blood spills into the night air as the cup hopelessly plummets into the sea. The essence of life scatters into oblivion.

A gold key hangs tied to the end of a long, wispy braid connected to the back of the woman's head. This shows that she possesses the solution to her own mental and emotional freedom. Unfortunately, the woman has lost sight of the key and has given up trying to find it. Although it is close by, the key lies out of the woman's narrow field of vision and she does not notice it. In order to rediscover it, she must turn her focus around. She will then be able to choose whether to unlock herself from this forlorn situation or remain as a voluntary prisoner.

In the distance, a ship takes advantage of the wind and sets its sail for adventure. It leaves the brooding young woman behind, never to pass her way again.

UPRIGHT MEANINGS:

When the Four of Cups comes up in a reading, this dispiriting card might indicate strong feelings of depression. Perhaps you are experiencing unhappiness in spite of your success. This could be because you focus too heavily on life's disappointments, and do not fully appreciate all you could be grateful for. Indifference has bled your sense of purpose, making it all too easy to cast vital things aside. Although you want nothing more than to feel happy and fulfilled, you somehow feel that you are undeserving of any such pleasure.

REVERSED MEANINGS:

When reversed, the Four of Cups strongly suggests that you unlock yourself from your emotional exile. New and exciting ideas are beginning to change your outlook on life. Realize that your cynical thinking has imprisoned you long enough. Snap out of your lethargic trance and finally seize the opportunities you have been disregarding. At this time, it is also vital to reconnect with your estranged relationships before they drift away for good.

"Four of Cups",
early sketch (2006)

In a preliminary design, a despondent youth dangles his feet over the ledge of a building. A small, moon-faced angel materializes in the sky above, offering the youth a golden chalice. The youth takes no notice of this heavenly gift because his depressing thoughts pull his attention downwards.

This concept would have worked well. However, I felt it would be too similar to the traditional imagery found in many other decks. Therefore, I eventually chose to depict someone who carelessly discards an inner blessing, instead of someone receiving a divine offering.

The old composition later became the basis for the Nine of Wands. In that card, the disheartened youth wears a bird mask to hide his face, and his poncho has evolved into idle wings. Unfortunately, the little angel holding the cup does not appear anywhere in the deck, but rumor has it that she might be seen fluttering around in an upcoming project.

The fortified tower seen in the Four of Cups was made with photos taken of a cottage-like mausoleum in Green-Wood Cemetery. This Romanesque vault is the eternal resting place of Lispenard Stewart, who was a wealthy New York politician in the late 1800s. He was interred here in 1927 at the age of 72.

Lispenard Stewart

267

THREE OF CUPS

Three merry souls celebrate their deliverance as they emerge from the mouth of a fearsome sea creature. Raising their golden goblets, the victorious trio cheerfully toasts their shared good fortune. Despite personality differences, they have overcome a dark situation by combining their strengths for a common purpose.

The nude harlot embodies the lust for life and its secular pleasures. Her passion and desire fueled her determination to break free of the beast. Unlike the surrounding salty ocean, the water streaming from the harlot's cup is pure and drinkable. She pours this water on her head, signifying that she has come out of darkness by absolving her own sins. This action also shows how one's clear thinking can determine a favorable destiny, regardless of a dubious past.

Two jovial characters sit on either side of the harlot. Both of these self-proclaimed holy men have put aside their contrasting philosophies, and discovered they are more alike than they initially assumed. The delighted clergyman in red feels indebted to his God for this miraculous salvation. He personifies the faith needed to keep believing in dreams when their realization seemed least likely. Opposite the clergyman sits a portly fellow disguised as a swami. The black mask he wears is a telltale sign that he is not a true man of religion, but merely an imposter and a swindler. Using deceit and a few underhanded magic tricks, he helped the trio connive their way out of peril.

The threesome not only escaped the horrific innards of the sea creature, but also managed to persuade the beast to rise up from the murky depths below. Free at last, they congratulate each other and rejoice in the moonlight; however, their carefree celebration may be premature. Their odyssey is not over, for they still remain stranded in the middle of the ocean. None of them has yet considered how to reach dry land. If they celebrate for too long, they give the sea creature time to change its mind and snap his deadly jaws shut.

Some who look at this card might conclude that the trio is descending into the beast, instead of rising out of it. In this interpretation, the threesome unites in mutual misfortune and decides to go down together happily, despite their differences. Accepting their mortality and living in the present moment, they celebrate their final moments of life.

UPRIGHT MEANINGS:

When the jolly Three of Cups surfaces in your reading, it often marks a well-deserved celebration amongst those who have prevailed together over adversity. Now is the time to breathe a sigh of relief and enjoy the success you have fought so hard to achieve. Applaud yourself as well as your partners over a job well done!

The Three of Cups may also symbolize the emotional bond forged between those caught in a crisis. These people will most likely become life-long comrades after their tribulation ends.

At this moment, you might still be in the throes of a harrowing ordeal. Know that you will soon fathom the means to escape this nightmare if you are persistent. Solutions to problems will become evident once you start cooperating with others. You might form an alliance with those you would not have considered trustworthy in the past. By working as a team, you will multiply your power, and surmount impossible odds with ease.

This favorable card may also represent a social get-together or festivities with friends. Make sure you associate with people who help bring your character up, not down.

Additionally, the Three of Cups could refer to ideas or dreams that have come to fruition after a monstrous struggle. Exult in the rewards that come from making your aspirations reality!

Reversed meanings:

There are several ways to interpret an inverted Three of Cups. Most of them deal with problems regarding interpersonal relationships.

You could be involved with a group that refuses to work harmoniously with each other. These difficult people constantly argue and refuse to rise above their differences. Power struggles, along with the deep-rooted dissention, sink your chances of success.

You might be compelled to obey the rigid will of a group. A narrow-minded committee lacking vision stifles your innovative spirit. Attempts to express yourself elicit the scorn of those who wish to drown your originality in a sea of conformity. Beware of succumbing to the negative influence of your peers. The card could be advising you to leave the pack and head out on your own.

In this topsy-turvy position, the Three of Cups can also represent overindulgence in your life. Furthermore, you may be fishing for shallow and immediate gratification instead of waiting for a delayed, but deeper reward.

In this early sketch, a trio of bald-headed women rejoices in triumphant celebration from their balcony, while a crowd of merry masqueraders revels below. Mingling in the festive crowd is a character that will retain his costume through various revisions of the card. Eventually, he will become the masked swami in the final version.

Although I did not complete the drawing, many of its elements went on to influence the creation of other cards in the deck. For instance, the balcony became the basis of composition in the Four of Cups, and the crowd of partygoers dwindled into the four happy children in the Six of Cups.

Initial design for Three of Cups, left

TWO OF CUPS

Two unlikely lovers stand together like a pair of ghosts inside a dreary room. On the left, the embodiment of Death wears a bold, red military jacket. The color and function of his uniform is telltale of his aggressive passion. The nude female on the right is the living manifestation of Midnight. Her skin complexion is dark and ethereal like the night sky, yet in some areas of her body, her coloring shifts from shades of black to light blue. This pigment variation signifies the deep, fluctuating nature of her emotions.

Death tempts Midnight with a curious proposition while seducing her with his sly charm. He uses devious words to confuse her mind, and then confiscates her trust with subtle persuasion. As Death declares his eternal love for Midnight, his soft funeral bandage reaches out and sensually wraps itself around her ankle. Once entangled, the delicate gauze will be harder to break than an iron chain.

The checkered floor is a symbolic reference to the game of chess. Like playing a game, Death uses cunning strategy to outwit Midnight's emotional defenses. He will checkmate her heart easily with a few well-planned moves.

Death blocks the door behind Midnight with his dirty hand and corners her into submission. He keeps her thoughts focused on his tantalizing promises so her mind will not wander and get lost in the world outside her window. Midnight disregards her instincts and finds herself weirdly attracted to Death. This ghoulish fascination causes the ends of her long black hair to light up with excitement.

Midnight finally concedes to Death's relentless advances and pledges her soul to him. Raising two golden cups, the newly betrothed couple toasts the bond of their union. Although they appear to celebrate in harmony, their crossed wrists are an omen of future conflict. Midnight may soon begin to realize that she has gotten more than she bargained for out of this cockeyed arrangement.

A crescent moon hangs in perfect balance over the heads of the engaged lovers, indicating that the power struggle between them has reached equilibrium. Like the ever-changing phases of the moon, however, this truce is only temporary. Midnight may soon have a shift in awareness, and begin to reconsider her reckless involvement with Death.

Looking through the arched windows, one can see the rotting remains of an abandoned city. Each dilapidated building stands like a tombstone in a lifeless cemetery. Amidst the decay, the old clock tower smolders with glowing energy as its bells peal the arrival of the midnight hour. When the chimes cease, the apparitions of Midnight and Death will vanish together into the silence.

UPRIGHT MEANINGS:

In the Deviant Moon Tarot, the Two of Cups conveys the inexplicable allure of someone who is dangerous to your well-being. Beware the irresistible darkness! You may be entangling yourself in a situation that does not serve your best interest. Take into account the unforeseen consequences of this risky association.

Additionally, this card might warn of a cursed future disguised behind a romantic proposal. It can also reveal how one may be considering marriage for the wrong reasons. Understand the difference between love and delusion.

On the other hand, the Two of Cups could signify the launch of a diverse and outlandish relationship. You might be forming strong emotional ties with someone under odd circumstances. Accept that love is strange and mysterious. Do not be repelled by fate's uncanny arrangements.

REVERSED MEANINGS:

When the Two of Cups appears in reverse, it strongly advises you to sever the bonds of an unhealthy relationship before they strangle you to death. It is high time to divorce yourself from a rotten situation. Realize that staying attached will only result in devastation and ruin.

In this position, the card can indicate broken trust, incompatibility, or a conflict of interest between you and your partner. You might be involved in an unbalanced relationship in which one partner exploits an unfair advantage over another. You may also be having difficulty communicating with your partner or connecting with them on an emotional level.

The initial design for the Two of Cups (shown at left) pictured a pair of newlyweds sitting on a bridge. Holding hands, they stare into each other's eyes and make a toast to a promising future. Above, the moon breathes its blessings onto their full chalices. The young woman is visibly pregnant and about to come to term.

MIDNIGHT TEMPTED BY DEATH

The final version of the Two of Cups was inspired by a teenage artwork of mine entitled "Midnight Tempted by Death". The piece shows Death as an elongated figure wearing a chef's hat and an apron. Skilled in the culinary arts of an abandoned city, Death offers the female incarnation of Midnight a rotted fish carcass stuck on a fork, along with an appetizing array of bones on a tray.

"Midnight Tempted by Death" was a massive collage made of painted papers. I used a corrosive chemical to give the walls in the background a special texture, which doomed the

"Midnight", scan from original (1985)

artwork to swift disintegration. It only lasted a little more than a decade before it started to fall apart. For some time, I kept pieces of it wedged inside of an art portfolio until those finally crumbled to bits, as well. All that survives today is a photograph of the piece and a few sketches.

Although blurry, this old photo shows the original piece encased in a gothic cabinet I built. With the doors closed, the outside resembled a black coffin. Embedded into the top was a clay relief of fossilized fish bones. To create the ramshackle buildings in the background, I cut up and manipulated pages out of a book on Renaissance paintings. This was an early precursor to the photo manipulations I would be doing years later for the Deviant Moon Tarot.

"Midnight", sketch (1984, Age 17)

"Tempted by Death", watercolor sketch (1983, Age 16)

"Midnight Tempted by Death" (1985)

The bird-skulled chef in this piece later became the pregnant mother in the original, hand-painted Death card.

277

ACE OF CUPS

A beautiful archangel lovingly cradles her magnificent chalice against her heart. Her warm, compassionate spirit invigorates the liquid held inside, changing ordinary water into an elixir of kindness. With a copious amount of love to share from her cup, the angel invites the deviant moon to sip of its essence. This act of charity humbles the mischievous orb, which has never before indulged in such a generous offering of earthly goodwill. Regardless of how much the thirsty moon drinks, it can never deplete the fullness of the bountiful chalice.

The archangel embodies the exquisite beauty of life. Her precious jewels and her gold adornments are an outward manifestation of her inner splendor. The golden spikes on her exquisite headpiece burst forth like rays of sunlight from her mind as they herald the rise of her spiritual awareness.

The archangel's sinuous gown flows like a stream of water over her body. This graceful attire is a physical expression of her emotions. Through the transparent silk, the glimpse of her moon-shaped nipple hints at the angel's potential for motherhood, along with her innate ability to nourish future offspring with tenderness and affection.

The universe has blessed the angel with elegant wings that allow her to reach unlimited heights when powered by love's glory. Although the angel seeks to spread her love to all, she also desires the intimacy of a close and personal relationship.

A small pearl dangles from each end of the angel's long blue braids. These tiny clues suggest that she may be an innocent bride. The slave bracelet worn on her hand is also symbolic of matrimony, meaning that someone she loves has recently bound her heart. One might also notice the crescent moon inked in red on her shoulder. Bequeathed by her lover, this lunar body brand clearly displays a commitment to everlasting love and passion.

UPRIGHT MEANINGS:

Open up your heart! In its purest essence, the Ace of Cups symbolizes the emotional overflow of love and happiness. Always remember that if you desire more love, you first must give love to others. Likewise, when you express beautiful feelings, you will naturally attract more beauty into your life.

The glorious Ace of Cups often marks the beginning of a loving and fruitful relationship. You will gain spiritual riches by emotionally connecting with another soul. This demonstrative bond could be with a new friend, relative or lover. It can even be with a total stranger in need of compassion. In a romantic situation, the burgeoning love you share with your partner has the potential to mature into a strong marriage.

The Ace of Cups might also be a sign of fertility. A blessed pregnancy, made by love, might soon occur. The card can also symbolize mental creativity and the conception of wonderful ideas.

REVERSED MEANINGS:

When a reader deals the Ace of Cups upside down, water should symbolically pour out of the angel's chalice, but it does not! Something unseen stops the liquid from spilling. This may be symbolic of your current emotional state. An unconscious barrier is preventing the flow of your innermost feelings and confining your passion for life. You might be having trouble expressing your love to someone special. Do not be surprised if this emotional blockage leaves your relationship stagnant and unfulfilled. Furthermore, an inverted Ace of Cups could mean that you or your partner is reluctant to commit to a long-term relationship.

Then again, the card in this position might indicate an overwhelming flood of lovesick emotions. You may find yourself hysterical after an abrupt end to a relationship. Although the downpour of tears seems impossible to stop, you must find the strength within to take control of your feelings.

THE QUEEN IN DEATH

Some may see the archangel's chalice as a cremation urn missing its lid. The dusty ashes it once held inside have miraculously changed into clean water. The engraving on the chalice depicts the funeral procession of a young queen. Four mournful men kiss the queen's limp body goodbye as they pass under the tears of a weeping moon. Blessed by her loved ones, the queen's spirit rises like mist from the chalice and makes its way up into the heavens. This engraving is not as somber as it seems, for it reminds us that love is the only way to transcend death.

Twin seahorse handles grace the sides of the chalice. These talismans are signs of protection to those who journey into the afterlife. The archangel, however, does not need to use these handles to hold the vessel. Instead, she caresses the chalice with her hands and feels the golden metal with her skin. She transfers heartfelt emotions into the water and energizes the departing spirit of the queen with love.

"The Queen in Death", pencil drawing (1984, Age 17)

Sketch for the chalice engraving

"The Queen in Death", crayon sketch (1982, Age 15)

The design engraved on the angel's chalice came from an improvised drawing made when I was a young teen. In this slightly abstracted piece, several moon-shaped beings cart the body of the lunar queen to its final place of rest. I believe this is the first time that a nude, bald-headed woman made an appearance in my art. She has been running amok throughout my imagination ever since.

The photographic source for the seahorse handles came from props I created out of clay.

Suit of Pentacles

Those that dwell in the city of Pentacles are industrious and persistent. These people are prosperous in life because they are committed to doing whatever it takes to manifest their ideas and desires into reality. Unfortunately, they sometimes place material gain over spiritual connectivity. This leaves them feeling poor inside, despite their earthly riches. Once they begin investing more time and love into their relationships, their lives will rise to an unprecedented level of happiness, peace and fulfillment.

King of Pentacles

The stout King of Pentacles proudly displays the silvery emblem of his industrial dynasty. He is a powerful individual, who has worked diligently through the years to attain his status. Unlike other kings, he does not rest on his riches. He involves himself in every aspect of his kingdom, from major to menial tasks. Being a perfectionist, he often toils inside the factories alongside common laborers, making sure each product meets his strict specifications.

The King's impressive crown of smokestacks shows that business is always foremost on his mind. Unfortunately, this preoccupation leaves little room for spirituality. The pressure gauge fixed in the crown's center signifies mental stress, which is inherent to his position as an executive. When the meter gets too high, the King releases steam by converting his tension into useful energy.

The King's mighty suit of armor conveys his steely determination to succeed. He has fought hard to build his empire, and he will do anything necessary to maintain it. However, underneath that worn exterior, there may be a woman dying to break free! Such femininities include a studded kilt, high-heeled shoes, earrings, polished fingernails, and the dainty way in which his pinky sticks up. These attributes subtly express his soft, caring nature, which he often has to hide when dealing with ruthless business competitors. One might also interpret the King as a female who has assumed masculine qualities in order to compete in a male dominated world.

Upright meanings:

The King of Pentacles signifies an enterprising figure who will likely become wealthy through his business ventures. This captain of industry is not only a strong administrator,

but he is also an authority in his field. He is a wise investor and is proficient in all types of financial matters. Learn all you can from this shrewd character! Always look for ways to capitalize on unique opportunities. Be sure to set high standards and demand nothing short of excellence from yourself and others. By practicing self-discipline and control, you will be successful in everything you do.

The card may also represent an organization that prospers because of skilled management. In a well-ordered establishment supervisors lead with integrity and strive to bring out the best in their workers.

Reversed meanings:

When reversed, the King of Pentacles often represents a materialistic person fueled by greed. Beware! This crook may try to swindle you out of your hard-earned money. He might disguise himself as an honest financial consultant or a sincere investor. On the other hand, perhaps you are the one who is corrupt. If so, you must realize that you are only cheating yourself. It is time to turn your dishonest values around, as your lust for gain will only cause you to lose your soul in the end!

In this position, the King might also symbolize business mismanagement. A once promising venture may fail because of inefficiency, fraud or unethical practices. The reversed card could also signify a supervisor who exploits his underlings for profit.

I originally intended to use Coins for this suit rather than Pentacles. The borders of the cards were to be royal purple, and the images would have pictured wealthy citizens dressed in 18th century fashions. However, by the time I began working on them, I realized that the opulent theme I had planned, as well as the color palette, would have been similar to what I already created in the Suit of Cups. At that point, a dark, gritty, industrialized premise seized my imagination. Decaying factories replaced Arabic style palaces, and a blackened color theme absorbed the jeweled colors in darkness.

King of Coins, early color study (2007), left

Queen of Pentacles

The gracious Queen of Pentacles revels in her luxurious lifestyle; however, she pities the impoverished citizens of her kingdom. Leaving the comforts of her industrial palace behind, she ventures out into the dreary street to get a firsthand look at the city. As she roams through the urban decay, she encounters a group of neglected dolls sitting in an alley. Hoping to ease their misery, she generously offers them her royal pentacle.

Although the Queen means well, she fails to watch where she is going and accidentally steps on one of the doll's legs. She may be hurting the ones she intends to help because she has not taken the time to discover their true needs. In reality, the unloved dolls need more than just a handout. They also need emotional support and to be valued by society.

Upright meanings:

The Queen of Pentacles represents a powerful person who shows genuine concern for the welfare of others. She brings good into the world by sharing her material blessings with those less fortunate. When she appears in your reading, she may be asking you to donate to a worthy cause. Open your heart as well as your wallet! Experience the joy and satisfaction that comes from giving. Now is the perfect time to make a liberal contribution to society.

The Queen may also signify a courteous hostess who loves to entertain by throwing lavish parties or fundraisers. She always observes proper etiquette when dealing with social, cultural or business situations. Brush up on your manners and follow her refined example. Be respectful to others and impress them with your politeness.

Lastly, the Queen might represent someone who successfully balances family and career. Like her, you must give attention to each area of your life in order for things to run smoothly.

Reversed meanings:

When the Queen appears in reverse, her priorities often get confused. All of her focus seems to be on work and she conveniently forgets her domestic responsibilities. She rarely spends time with family or friends because she is so busy chasing her materialistic desires. Like her, you may not be giving enough of yourself to others. Know that there are souls out there starving for your attention. In order to feel fulfilled, you must invest more in your relationships.

On the other hand, you may be giving so much to others that you neglect your own needs. Remember, if you do not take care of yourself first, you will have nothing worth giving to anyone else.

Maybe your controlling personality makes you try to do everything for everybody. All this doting might make you feel important, but you must realize that you have become overbearing. Although unintentional, you are emotionally suffocating your loved ones. You

7/23/07

need to step back and give them room to breathe. You have to accept the fact that they are more than capable of looking after themselves.

Finally, the reversed Queen could represent a vulgar person who has horrible manners.

In this early design, the Queen breaks her golden coin in half and offers the pieces to her needy dolls.

Photos taken of an ordinary vacuum cleaner hose were used to create the dolls' legs. Their golden feet were made from doorknobs.

Queen of Coins, early design (2007), left

Knight of Pentacles

The diligent Knight of Pentacles slowly patrols the factory courtyards in an endless cycle. His metal wheels grind along the same path every evening, cutting a groove that keeps him on track. Although his duties are unerringly mundane, he has no desire to venture out and explore the unknown parts of the city. He would rather remain in familiar territory, where he knows what to expect around every corner.

The Knight is an unwavering professional who performs at the highest level. He flaunts an upright pentacle, which he earned by consistently working hard throughout the years. His iron armor reflects his industrious nature while giving him the appearance of a steam locomotive. The three red whistles equipped on the back of his helmet help him stick to a predictable work schedule. There is also an exhaust pipe fixed to his rear, which allows him to eliminate the nonessentials from his life and maximize efficiency.

Upright meanings:

The Knight of Pentacles symbolizes the methodical work ethic needed in order to achieve success. Like him, you must be patient as well as persistent. Never rush through the tasks set before you. Complete them all with meticulous care, regardless of how long it takes. Be sure to develop regular habits that will help you move towards a worthy destiny.

In a financial situation, the card may be advising you to be cautious with your money. Understand that there is no quick and easy track to wealth. Avoid the risks! Seek conservative investments with a slow but steady yield. For the ultimate payoff, you must remember to take stock in yourself, as well as your enterprises. The Knight may also characterize someone who has ritualistic behaviors or obsessions.

Reversed meanings:

When the overturned Knight appears in your reading, it might mean that you are stuck in a rut. Life feels utterly boring and monotonous. Nothing seems to move you lately. Maybe you are engaged in repetitive work that dulls your mind and drains the energy from your body. In order to break free, you must dare to drive yourself in a new direction. Stop following the same tedious routine and start doing something different for a change.

Additionally, the reversed Knight could represent an irresponsible person who habitually shirks his duties. He may also symbolize inconsistent or unreliable performance.

This early design of the Knight pictures a blue-faced creature encased in armor. The creature later became the tattooed painter in the Three of Pentacles.

Knight of Coins, ink sketch (2007)

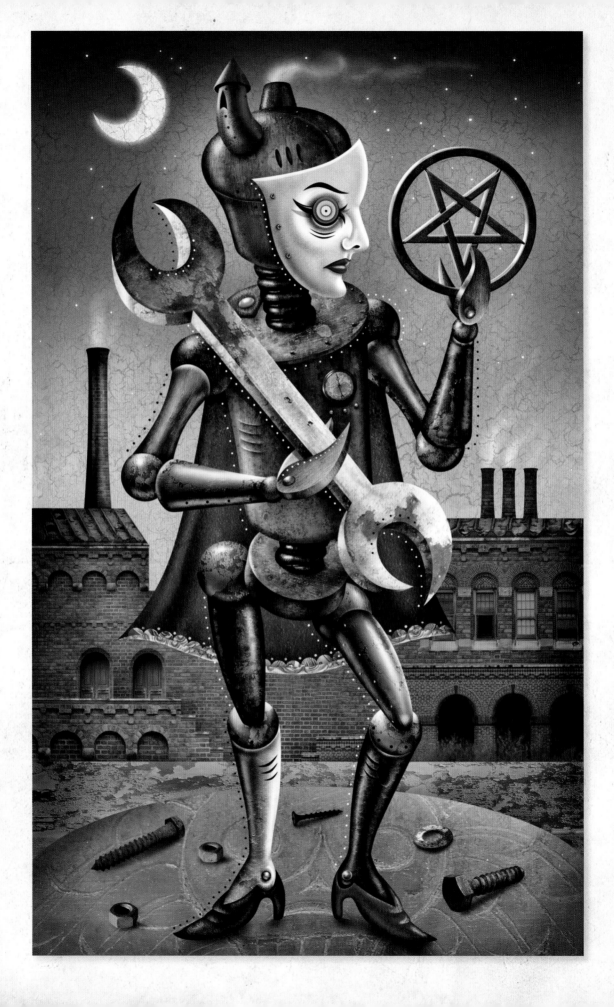

Page of Pentacles

The scholarly Page reflects upon a rusted old pentacle he has found in a scrap pile. He has built himself with spare parts like this and recognizes the value of such a remarkable discovery. While this pentacle is not as refined as those owned by the rest of the royal family, it validates the unique rewards that can only be attained though self-improvement.

At this point in time, the unfinished Page is merely a metallic skeleton. He is just beginning to flesh out the features of his evolving character. The mask he wears implies that he may be trying on different personalities, knowing that he will eventually find the right one to suit his needs.

Being resourceful, the Page sees vast possibilities in every situation. He makes use of whatever comes his way, regardless of the condition. Nevertheless, he is selective about what becomes a part of him. He will reject anything that does not fit into his blueprint for success, as suggested by the discarded bits of hardware scattered at his feet.

Steam pours from a small exhaust vent on top of the Page's head, revealing that the gears of his inventive mind are in motion. Although he produces brilliant ideas, they are useless without action. For this reason, he has equipped himself with pinchers that enable him to craft his priceless thoughts into reality.

The Page carries an enormous wrench that symbolizes his ever-growing skills. With this powerful tool, he has the potential to construct his own destiny. His emerging talents will provide him with unlimited options for the future. However, his mismatched shoes indicate that he is still trying to decide on which direction to travel in life.

Upright meanings:

The Page of Pentacles often represents a curious student who is eager to learn. This enterprising individual puts his studies to practical use and creates his own opportunities. Take in all you can from his example and make yourself more valuable to the world. Know that you have the power to develop yourself and become whoever you want to be. Be sure to make the most of the resources available to you, no matter how crude or limited.

In terms of higher education, the card may be a sign of an upcoming grant or scholarship. It could also signify someone who is self-taught. The young Page might also represent the initial phase of a business venture or project. Innovative ideas are coming together from various sources to form a whole new entity. Additionally, the Page could be advising you to work your body and improve your overall health.

Reversed meanings:

When reversed, the Page of Pentacles might represent an adolescent who is not properly preparing himself for the future. This naive youth often daydreams about the things he

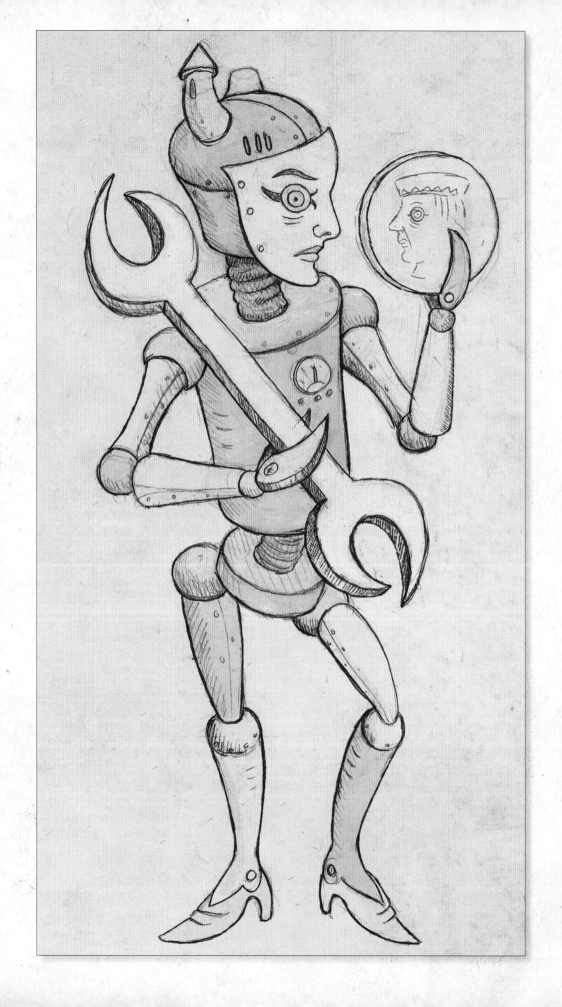

wants out of life, yet he fails to do what is hard and necessary to achieve them. Like him, you may not be fully committed to your ambitions. In your immaturity, you tend to seek immediate pleasure without considering the substantial benefits of delayed gratification. Sadly, your lack of foresight and self-discipline will ultimately lead to tremendous regret.

In this position, the card can also refer to obstacles that may be preventing someone from pursuing further education. Examples of such hindrances include poverty, self-doubt or laziness.

Page of Pentacles, preliminary study (2007)

Sketch for a more cultured looking character (2007), left

TEN OF PENTACLES

A wealthy father schools his son in a game of chess, imparting his knowledge not only of the game, but of life, as well. Being an intelligent mentor, he trains the boy to evaluate problems, think ahead, and formulate successful solutions on his own. With more time and experience, the child will ultimately become a master.

The father leans on a wooden cane, which signifies that he is much older than his son. When he joins his ancestors in death, his son will assume the role of patriarch and carry on the family's heritage. From above, the spirits of their forefathers proudly watch over them in the form of stone carvings on the wall.

Ten pentacles create an arc around the background window, framing the boy's future inheritance. Looking out into the courtyard, one can see a thriving factory churning in the distance. An illuminated path leads to a golden door, which will eventually open for the boy once he is old enough to take charge of his father's enterprise. The crescent moon hanging over the rooftops brings a sense of balance and stability into the scene.

The chessboard rests on the back of an obedient blue servant. This suggests that the father may have built his fortune off the sweat of his laborers. Unbeknownst to the father and his son, the servant has quietly stolen the king piece, thus she holds the true power in this situation, regardless of her inferior position. If she simply stood up, the board and all the pieces would come crashing to the ground.

UPRIGHT MEANINGS:

The Ten of Pentacles represents the sharing of family values and traditions through the generations. It is also about connecting with your ancestral lineage and leaving a lasting legacy behind for your descendants to follow. If you are an adult, make it your responsibility to pass your wisdom down to the young. Guide them with your experience, but let them learn from their own mistakes. If you happen to be a young person, it would behoove you to take advice from your elders and use it to your advantage.

This card may also symbolize the satisfying result of a lifetime of hard work and achievement. Perhaps you have accumulated sizable wealth over the years, both financially and in your relationships. Use this golden time to relax with your loved ones while enjoying the bounty of your assets. If you have not yet reached this noble stage of life, know that you can reap similar rewards in the future through strategic investments and partnerships.

REVERSED MEANINGS:

In reverse, the Ten of Pentacles warns that you may one day live in poverty as a result of a lifetime of poor financial planning and neglect. If you want to have economic security in your later years, you must stop squandering your time and money today. Know that you are never too young to start preparing for your long-term future.

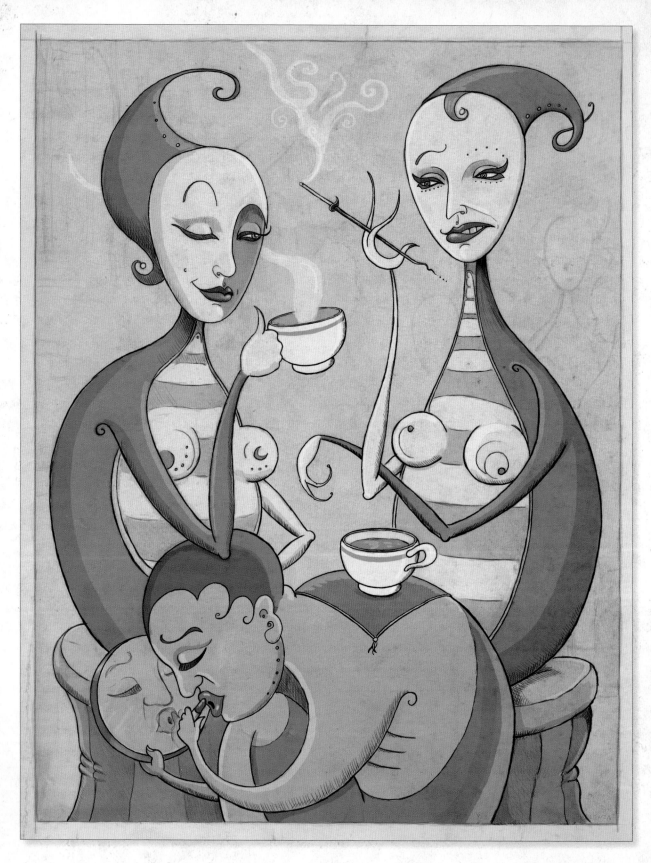

The blue servant hiding under the chessboard originally served as a human coffee table in this pre-Deviant Moon sketch. Set in an outside café, the drawing shows the servant applying the lipstick she stole from the two fashionable patrons.

In this position, the card could also allude to unfortunate family matters. Such issues could pertain to a legal dispute over a relative's will, or an upsetting family secret that is ready to surface. Furthermore, it might signify relatives who cheat one another and refuse to live by the rules.

THE GAME OF KINGS

My father taught me how to play chess when I was three years old. Throughout my childhood, the game was our special way of spending time together. He was a serious player, yet I often daydreamed over the pieces while waiting for him to make a move. In my imagination, each was a fanciful character in a grand story. I remember pretending that the bishops were nuns and the pawns were the orphans left in their care. Sometimes, I made the nuns line the children up and take them to feed the horses, which were dutifully played by the knights.

White side

Black side

Ever since those early days, I have wanted to make a figurative chess set of my own. I once tried to carve a set out of wood, but quickly discovered it would take years to develop the necessary skills to do so. Years later, I tried sculpting detailed pieces out of terra cotta and casting them into molds, but that turned out to be a disaster. I finally found the right method while teaching a group of seven-year-old art students how to form clay space aliens with their fingers. Using this natural approach, I created the primitive set pictured in the Ten of Pentacles out of fired porcelain.

The Deviant Moon chess set is massive. The king measures ten inches tall with a base that is almost three inches in diameter. Each hand-formed piece has its own quirky personality. Unfortunately, I never made a board gigantic enough to hold them all. Although the set is not practical for play, it remains an impressive sight to behold.

The stolen king piece

301

Nine of Pentacles

An elegant woman strolls through the city streets accompanied by her winged pet. Although she comes from a humble part of town, she is well on her way to greater things. Her wheeled foot indicates that she is moving with ease through the hierarchy of society. The factory in the background symbolizes her industrious work ethic, which she uses to bridge the gap between poverty and prosperity. Nine pentacles glide down from the sky, showering her in a display of material wealth and abundance.

The woman's stylish but strange figure reveals much about her character. Her armless torso suggests that she no longer needs to work because she has reached financial independence. She also wears a fine silk dress, which reflects her expensive taste. Her mask shows that she has taken on a new identity in order to fit in with the pretentious upper class. It could also express her individuality and her potential to become whoever or whatever she wishes to be.

The woman keeps her mischievous pet on an unbreakable chain leash. This could mean that she has restrained the dark side of her personality in order to get ahead in life. Another interpretation could be that her lavish lifestyle leaves her chained to eternal debt. Furthermore, the winged skull may symbolize her inescapable mortality. Regardless of her earthly riches, she will ultimately share the same fate as the pauper.

An alternative analysis of the card suggests that the fashionable woman is a spoiled diva. The black mask she wears might then represent her phony personality. The absence of arms implies that she is merely a useless societal ornament. Her wealth may come from a trust fund, a divorce settlement, or from the sweat of those she exploits.

Upright meanings:

The Nine of Pentacles represents someone of sophistication and refinement. This self-sufficient person maintains a high standard of living and enjoys surrounding herself in luxury. Like her, you may have attained an incredible level of material success. Well done! Your disciplined efforts have compounded to bring you fantastic rewards. It is time to bask in the golden glow of victory, knowing that you have earned the right to enjoy the bounty of your labor.

If you have not yet reached the success you dream of, the card advises you to keep going day by day. Although your journey may be difficult, you must stay confident and continue to work hard. Do not lose sight of the grand vision you have for yourself. Think of all the fabulous rewards awaiting you.

Reversed meanings:

Unfortunately, the reversed Nine of Pentacles card could be an indicator of a financial upheaval. You might suddenly find yourself without a source of income, making it difficult

for you to maintain a comfortable lifestyle. Unforeseen expenses could drain your bank account. You may have to sell off your valuable possessions just to survive.

In this position, the card could also warn that you are living beyond your means. Understand that your extravagant taste will only lead to poverty in the end. It is time to reduce your expenses and develop a thrifty budget. You will never accumulate real wealth unless you control your frivolous spending and start investing your money for the future.

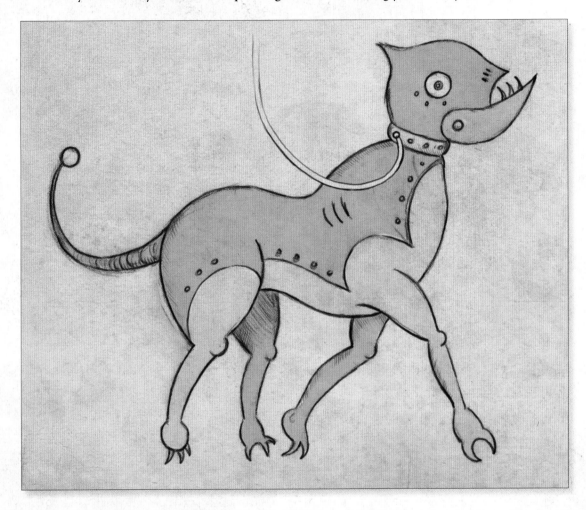

Early idea for an iron pet sketch (2007)

THE WALKING LADY

The Walking Lady first appeared in one of my elementary school art projects. I based her attire on what we were learning about Japanese culture at the time. Her short silk dress gives her a modern flair along with her white stockings and high heel slippers. The mask she wears evolved from my botched attempt at painting her black hair, yet she still managed to keep her Geisha girl hairpins in the end. The reason I left her armless remains a mystery.

Watercolor (1979, Age 12), left

Eight of Pentacles

Deep inside the bowels of an old factory, a lone worker toils through the night manufacturing a set of eight extraordinary pentacles. He begins production by tugging on a cable that releases molten globs of gold into a system of pipes. The metallic liquid then oozes through the workings of a giant machine, where it is molded and pressed into its final shape. One by one, the worker's goods roll down the conveyor belt, tempered by the heat of the furnace fire.

Always vigilant in his craftsmanship, the worker tolerates nothing less than perfection. Although this first batch meets his strict approval, he will not pause to celebrate his success. Instead, he will continue to work until dawn, and strive to make the next series of pentacles better than the last.

The machine represents the laborious process of turning a raw thought into a tangible object. However, it would be nothing more than a scrap pile without the worker actively taking part in its operation. With his guidance, the rusted gears mimic the synchronized rotation of the heavens. The deities embodied in the cogs look favorably upon the worker, rewarding his tireless dedication with the means to create limitless prosperity and abundance.

Upright meanings:

The Eight of Pentacles represents some of the character traits you will need in order to produce the very best in life. Like the dedicated worker pictured on the card, you must be willing to grind without rest until your project is complete. Keep in mind that you are a professional. Discipline yourself to do what must be done whether you want to do it or not. Fully concentrate on the task at hand and pay close attention to the details. Be patient and persistent in your efforts until you achieve the flawless results you desire.

The card shows both a clock and a pressure gauge in the background. This could mean that you are working under tremendous stress in order to meet a deadline or to fulfill a quota. Regardless of the difficulty, you must maintain consistency in your work. Never skimp when it comes to quality. Be prepared to reject anything that falls short of excellence.

Reversed meanings:

When reversed, the Eight of Pentacles may suggest that your work is of inferior quality. This could be because of carelessness, laziness or your inability to keep up with demand. Perhaps you need to manage your time better and become more organized. You might also consider upgrading your skills in order to meet the high standards expected of you.

Additionally, you may be so obsessed with perfection that you hardly produce anything at all for fear of making a mistake. You might also be focusing on aspects of your work that contribute little to your overall success.

Finally, the card may indicate that you are looking for a quick and easy path to success. Know that you will never achieve anything worthwhile as long as you avoid the backbreaking work required to fulfill your dreams.

"The Carpenter Working on a Coffin", early sketch for the Eight of Coins (2007)

Inspiration for the machine found in the Eight of Pentacles came from one of my favorite teenage drawings. In this overly busy illustration, a team of robots labor to produce more of their own kind out of old toasters, telephones and televisions.

"The Machine" (Age 16), left

Seven of Pentacles

The young witch practices her spells in the factory garden. Sticking a black tree with a rusty nail, she evaluates the growth of her skill. A large drop of blood oozes from the puncture wound and slowly drips down the slick bark. The red-stained grass at the roots indicates that she has performed this painful ritual many times before. Seven small pentacles bloom from the tree's once dead branches, giving the witch the incentive to persist with her studies. As her power matures, the tree will yield grander gifts in greater abundance.

The blood is symbolic of the sacrifices one must make when cultivating a talent, the demands of which are often terribly draining. The tapped blood will not go to waste, for as it seeps into the ground it nourishes the roots below and feeds the entire tree in a perpetual cycle. This metaphor shows that one must continually invest in oneself in order to flourish.

The tree represents the various stages of skill development. The roots serve as the starting point for an amateur working her way up to the rewards on the branches. The witch pokes the tree at midpoint, indicating that she is neither a beginner nor an expert, but someone of average ability. With dedication and consistent effort, she will one day master her craft.

Upright meanings:

When the Seven of Pentacles appears in your reading, it recommends that you take a moment to evaluate your progress in any given area. Check to see if your ambitions are still on course and make adjustments if needed. Give yourself credit for all that you have done up until this point, and consider all that you want to achieve in the days ahead.

If you are working to develop new skills, you may have noticed tremendous growth in your ability lately. Congratulations! Your diligent effort is starting to pay off. Enjoy the fruits of your labor, knowing that even greater compensation is yet to come. Be advised, however, that this is not the time to sit back and relax. Your dreams still require constant nurturing and attention. You must push yourself harder than ever before to make them all come true.

Reversed meanings:

When reversed, the Seven of Pentacles symbolizes the impatience or frustration one might feel when learning a challenging new skill. Despite your best efforts, it seems that you are making little progress. As discouragement sets in, you will likely begin to doubt your abilities, as well as your worth. The card could also indicate that you are trying to rush something before it is ready, or that you want to give up on something prematurely.

Whatever the case may be, it is necessary to remain patient. Understand that what you have been working on needs more time to develop.

In addition, the reversed card could suggest that a project or undertaking may fail due to a lack of commitment. Failure might also come because those involved have not laid the proper groundwork in the beginning to ensure strong and steady growth.

A rusty nail often signifies slow progress or laziness. The witch uses such a nail to show that she has learned how to handle resistance and procrastination.

Early witch drawing (1975, Age 8)

THE WITCH IN THE WALL

When my mother was a child, she used to tell her younger siblings that an evil witch lived in their bedroom wall. She told the toddlers that if they misbehaved during the day, the witch would come out at midnight and pull them into the wall to live with her forever. She told the same story to me when I was growing up, but it never frightened me. I truly wanted to meet the witch in person! I remember pressing my ear against the sheetrock, hoping to hear her moving around inside. I imagined her living in a spacious purple room behind the wall, singing to her pet bat while mixing mysterious potions in her cauldron.

"Little Witch with Two Tails", sketch (2007), left

Six of Pentacles

Compassion for the plight of the dead has led a wealthy man into the cemetery. As he walks along a row of mausoleums, he meets a lowly spirit who longs for the material world. Clutching the man's leg, the spirit begs for something tangible to take back to his tomb. A slender white arm emerges from a window in the man's chest, offering one of six pentacles in an open display of generosity.

Situated high upon a granite platform, the wealthy man overlooks the needy spirit below. This contrast in elevation illustrates and compares their status in society. One dominates from a position of economic power while the other is dependent and submissive.

The man's red torso resembles the tower of a fortified building. This could mean that he embodies an institution that lends or distributes money, such as a bank, the government or a charitable organization. Standing on three legs in front of a large pillar intensifies the man's aura of financial stability. The five pentacles he holds behind his back indicate that he has a reserve fortune that can last a lifetime and sustain many.

Upright meanings:

The Six of Pentacles often represents the transference of money or material possessions from one person to another; however, it could pertain to a spiritual exchange, as well. When this card appears in a reading, it is vital to determine if you are being portrayed as the giver or the recipient.

As the giver, you may feel inclined to share your resources with those less fortunate. The universe has blessed you in so many ways, and now is the time to pay it forward. While there is no obligation to do so, consider making a bountiful contribution to a worthy cause, or simply extend a little support to an impoverished soul. Perform these altruistic deeds from the goodness of your heart, and do not be concerned with compensation. The more you give of yourself, the richer life becomes.

If you are receiving charity, it would be proper to express gratitude to your benefactor. However, you must not rely on this assistance for too long. Find ways to rise above the destitution instead of begging for support. Know that you will never have true control over your life if you are perpetually indebted to someone else.

"Wealthy Man with Coins",
preliminary design (2007)

"Six of Coins" (2007)

Reversed meanings:

In reverse, the Six of Pentacles could mean that someone is looking to take advantage of your kindness. Though you want to help your fellow man, you must be cautious at this time. Do not be duped by a devious scam. Think twice before you make any donations.

On the other hand, the reversed card might be a warning not to accept a certain gift or favor. What appears to be an act of goodwill could have strings attached. You may be expected to pay more than you bargained for in return.

The Six of Pentacles, formerly the Six of Coins, is the only card in the deck to have a completed alternate version. In this variation, a citizen with an elephant trunk made of bricks emerges from the factory and presents a golden coin to the crowd below. Although some in the crowd are truly in need, the two-headed woman in yellow prospers from society's handouts and entitlements. Her three hands show that she is eager to grab whatever windfall comes her way.

When I finished making this card, I realized that its whimsical characters strayed too far from those found in the rest of the deck. Although I reworked the entire design, the original idea of a benefactor giving charity from a ledge survived in the end. The backdrop switched from an industrial setting to a dreary graveyard, and the woman in yellow was transformed into the pleading ghost.

Pennies from the Dead

The idea of a wealthy man giving alms to the dead came from a curious experience I had as a child while playing in a cemetery. A friend and I were out exploring the tombs one day when we spotted a trail of pennies scattered across a dozen graves. Believing they were a gift from our spirit friends, we gathered the coins up and counted them out with excitement. (The total amount came to 111, a number that has had strange significance for me ever since.) We took the eerie pennies home and placed them in a tin cup, calling our loot the deadly treasure.

I wound up holding on to the pennies through the years and always considered them as a sign of good fortune. As I reached adulthood and gained success in life, I decided to return to the old cemetery to repay my ghostly loan with interest. When I found the original graves of prosperity, I spread 111 silvery nickels over them and humbly thanked the spirits below for investing in my imagination.

"Begging Spirit", sketch (2007)

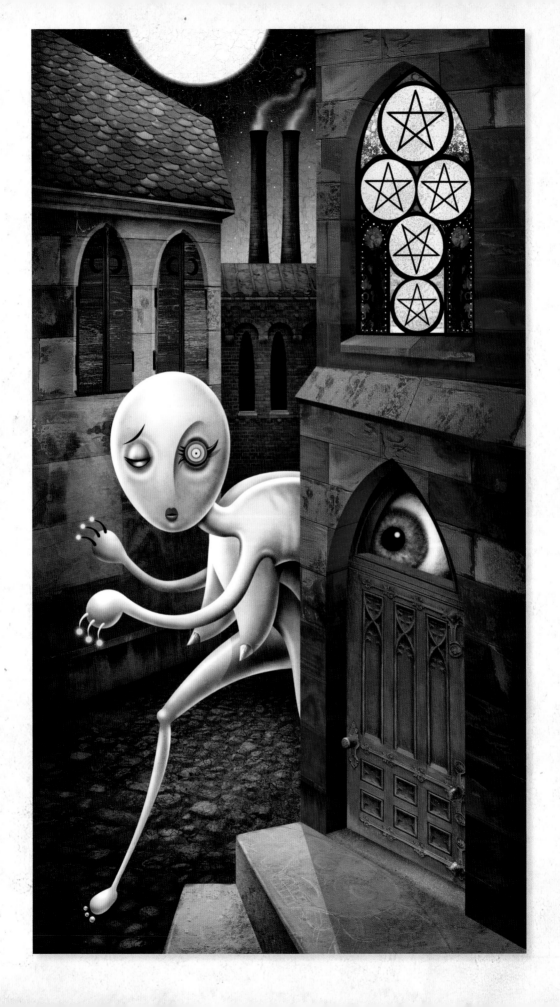

FIVE OF PENTACLES

A lady of the night leaves the wicked factory behind and flees through the narrow streets of the city. Having none of the city's amenities, she searches for sanctuary amidst a maze of soulless industrial buildings. Shadows from her past chase her along the way, trying to convince her that she is unworthy of redemption. From above, a full moon looms over her head, bearing the heavy weight of her guilty conscience. Footsore and weary, the lady finally discovers hope in the form of five pentacles glowing in a stained-glass church window.

Although the penitent lady is in dire need, the closed church door implies that she is unwelcome in this holy house. Those who dwell behind the door have locked it tight in order to keep out the darkness. A probing eyeball peers through the hatch and scrutinizes the lady, contemplating whether or not to let someone like her inside.

One should not be so quick to pass moral judgment on this lost soul without first considering her situation. Living in extreme poverty, she may have sold herself to the night simply to survive. Perhaps she used sex as a currency because she had nothing else to bargain with. Besides the sexual connotations, her bare breasts could also symbolize motherhood and the possibility that she has hungry children to feed. The card implies that she is doing all she can to move herself into the light of mercy. At this critical moment, she needs assistance, not a lecture on decency.

UPRIGHT MEANINGS:

The Five of Pentacles could represent a bitter period of financial adversity. Unfortunately, you might suddenly find yourself unemployed or penniless. Be warned that you will likely have difficulty getting work for quite a while. With no viable source of income, you may be cast out into the street and compelled to seek charity from others.

The card might also mean that it is time to escape poor working conditions in order to discover bright opportunities. Know that you deserve so much more! The ideal job is out there, but you must look long and hard to find it. Have no fear as you make the rocky transition from scarcity to abundance.

Finally, the Five of Pentacles sometimes suggests social rejection or abandonment. Maybe you are having trouble getting into an exclusive organization, or perhaps you are the one responsible for leaving others out in the cold. Additionally, the card could represent someone who has fallen from grace and now desperately seeks forgiveness. It might also signify someone longing to reconnect with her spirituality.

"Stalked in the Catacombs", crayon drawing (Circa 1980, Age 13?)

"Twisted Alleyway—Midnight and Sunrise", pastel (Circa 1983, Age 16)

When reversed, the Five of Pentacles predicts an end to your economic or spiritual destitution. Take comfort in knowing that better times are just around the corner. Salvation may come by finding new employment or by connecting with people who genuinely care about your welfare. Furthermore, you may finally be accepted into a social group that once ostracized or condemned you for your transgressions. Remember to accept yourself first, regardless of your perceived faults or past mistakes.

The lady portrayed in the Five of Pentacles originated in one of my early teenage drawings. The sketch shows a woman made of shapes running away from two shadowy figures. A third shadowy figure hides in a doorway waiting to ambush the terrified woman as she passes.

The street scene pictured in the Five of Pentacles was inspired by one of my old high school art projects. The assignment was to render an imaginary cityscape during both night and day. When designing the card, I wanted to recreate these warped buildings to emphasize the lady's distorted mental state. However, I eventually straightened them out in favor of a tighter composition.

The lady of the night is the same woman seen in the Lover's card. Sadly, she has physically declined after years of hard living.

Five of Coins, rough sketch (2007)

Four of Pentacles

Agrotesque demon escorts a wicked miser from his counting house and leads him into the roaring flames of damnation. Afraid to face his doom, the miser looks back in anguish over the life he leaves behind. As he reflects upon his past, a sinister claw grabs his shoulder to remind him of all his misdeeds and mistakes.

Regardless of his staggering wealth, the miser's money cannot buy another day. He begs the demon for more time to tend to unfinished business, but the broken pocket watch dangling from her rotted mouth shows there is no more left to give.

With one boot missing, the miser marches into the furnace unprepared. He foolishly clutches four golden pentacles in a desperate attempt to maintain his worldly possessions. Even in his hour of death, he would rather cuddle his cold fortune than embrace the warmth of another human being. The shadows of eager hands slither up his robe, yearning to snatch his treasure once his blackened carcass lies shriveling in the fire.

Upright meanings:

The Four of Pentacles illustrates the ugly consequence of putting material gain above all else. Like the miser portrayed in the card, your greed and selfishness may be steering you towards a future filled with regret. In the end, it will not matter how much money you have or how many things you possess. Your value will ultimately be measured by how much you have loved and how much you have been loved.

Although there is nothing wrong with the pursuit of wealth, it is important to remember that you can never truly own anything in life, for the treasures you cling to today will one day belong to another.

In addition, the Four of Pentacles could symbolize the fear of losing all that you worked hard for. It could also represent the apprehension one might feel when confronted by his own mortality or a sudden life-changing event.

Reversed meanings:

When the Four of Pentacles appears in reverse, it may mean that you will soon experience a profound shift in your values. Life will take on new meaning once you reorder your priorities and focus on your greater purpose. Know that there is more to you than just your material possessions. Regardless of how much you have acquired, it will never be enough to fulfill you. Unless you invest in your spirit, something will always be missing deep inside. Keep in mind that time is your greatest commodity. Spend it freely on your loved ones while you still can and create precious memories that will last into eternity.

The Ultimate Failure

I based the story behind the Four of Pentacles on an extremely self-centered relative I once had. This materialistic man's entire life revolved around his possessions. He spent most of his days obsessing over money, and he routinely put his wants above his children's needs. Death took him by surprise one cold December morning around 9:40 am. (In the card, the watch hanging from the demon's mouth displays the identical time.) Nobody was particularly heartbroken when they heard the news. I could not help but imagine him lying frozen in the morgue on his way to cremation. Were the thoughts inside his lifeless skull screaming, "I wish I spent more time with my children as they grew up", or "Damn, I wish I spent more time at the office"?

Besides leaving his grown children a legacy of resentment towards him, this egoistic relative also left them his ashes inside a luxurious urn. As one might have guessed, none of his children wanted to keep this ghastly trophy of selfishness in their homes. What they wished to have most of all were photographs of their father actively participating in their lives through the years, but sadly, such priceless treasures did not exist.

Four of Coins, preliminary sketch (2007), left

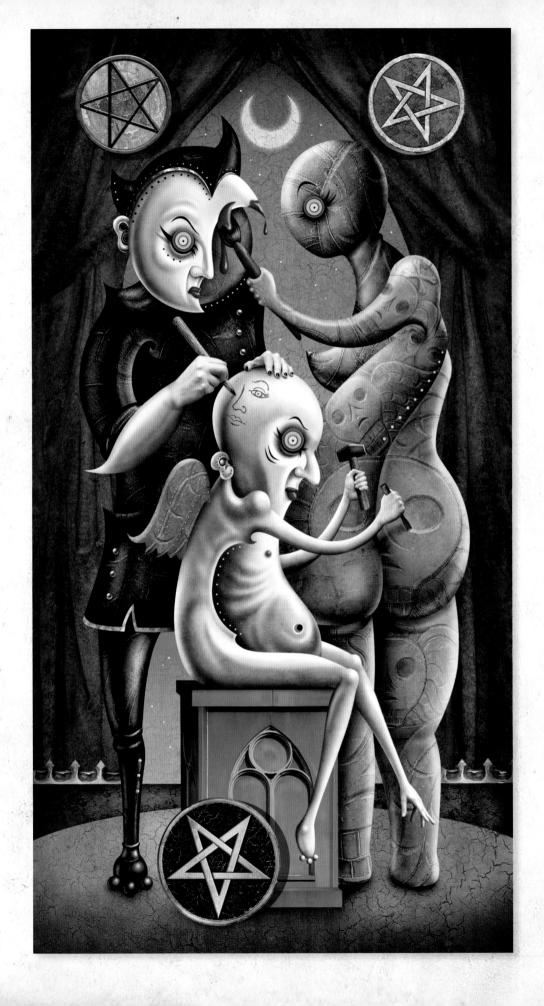

THREE OF PENTACLES

Three talented artisans are busy at work in the studio. Together they combine their diverse skills to create an unforgettable masterpiece. Each of them influences the other's style in an invaluable way. The artist dressed in black expertly draws a portrait on the bald head of an angel seated on a pedestal. This inspires the angel to chisel his dark feelings into the blue skin of a female model. The female maintains this never-ending cycle of creativity by painting over the eye of the artist, coloring his view of reality.

Although the artisans act as a unified team, their unique personalities still come through in their creations. The three distinctive pentacles displayed in the studio represent their dedication to craft, as well as their individuality. In the background, the parted curtains reveal a crescent moon hanging in perfect balance. This metaphor shows that the artisans have pushed their egos aside and opened their minds to universal intuition.

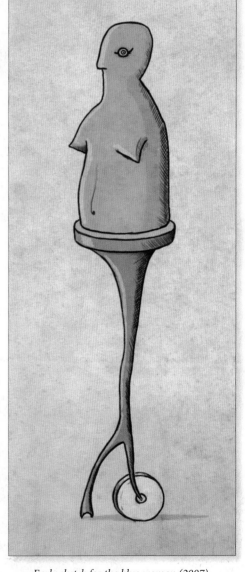

UPRIGHT MEANINGS:

The Three of Pentacles represents the concentrated efforts of a synchronized team. Like the artists pictured on the card, it is time for you to collaborate with others in a creative environment. Freely contribute your talents to the group and learn all you can from your fellow workers. Collectively, you will multiply your productivity and get results that would be impossible to achieve alone.

In addition, this card symbolizes the quest for excellence in one's work. Always strive for quality, yet do not be overly concerned with perfection. Put everything you have into the task at hand along with a little extra. Know that your projects will require serious planning and coordination in order to reach completion.

REVERSED MEANINGS:

When reversed, the Three of Pentacles is a disappointing sign of mediocrity and poor craftsmanship. For some reason, you are not making your best work anymore. Perhaps you've lowered your standards or developed

Early sketch for the blue woman (2007)

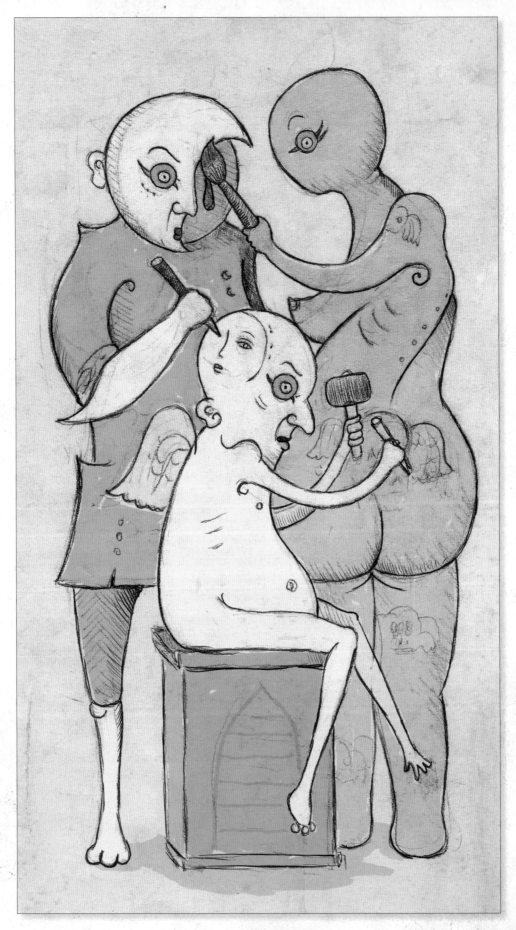

"Three Artisans", sketch (2007)

inefficient work habits. Stop performing below your capability! It is time to refocus your efforts and get back into a creative flow.

In this position, the card can also represent a creative conflict within an organization. Unfortunately, this group never produces anything worthy because its members are only in it for themselves. If you work with difficult colleagues like these, it may be better if you leave to find a more harmonious team with whom to collaborate.

To make the angel's pedestal, I used photos of the Gothic paneling found on top of the Nassau County Veterans Memorial at Eisenhower Park, N.Y.

Two of Pentacles

The mysterious belly dancer performs under the light of a crescent moon balancing two pentacles against the sky. With uncanny style, she slinks across the carpet and shakes her hips to a hauntingly sensual melody. A mesmerized audience watches in awe as she skillfully juggles the silvery pentacles from one hand to the other. Although her agile moves seem effortless, they come with great practice and concentration.

As the drums quicken to a maddening beat, the dancer feverishly spins her head while whipping her braided tendrils through the air. Her pulsating shimmies cause the silver on her leather costume to jingle in a wild rhythmical tempest. On the back of her studded belt, a jeweled, red skull swings with the gyration and grins with crazed delight.

Without warning, the music comes to a sudden stop, and the night is still once more. The winded belly dancer strikes a final pose before silence erupts into frenetic applause.

Upright meanings:

The Two of Pentacles represents balance and harmony with effort. Perhaps you are trying to manage two momentous areas of life at once. This is never an easy task. In order for things to flow smoothly, you will need to utilize all of your talents and adapt to shifting situations. Always stay focused and keep on your toes. Work hard, yet remain graceful regardless of the difficulty. One clumsy move and everything you have tried to uphold may come crashing down!

This opulent card may also signify a rewarding business partnership, as well as a period of hard-earned financial stability.

Reversed meanings:

When reversed, the Two of Pentacles symbolizes the inability to maintain balance in one's life. While you are doing your best to handle everything, you are neglecting what matters most. It is time to drop unimportant things so you can focus solely on your top priorities.

In this position, the card can also indicate difficulty in making a weighty choice. The fear of taking a false step keeps you immobilized. Do not let this indecision tear you in two! Perhaps you need to consider a third option.

In addition, the reversed card might mean that you are having trouble managing your finances. Learn how to budget your money more efficiently so you can turn this lopsided situation around.

Two of Coins, early concept sketches (2007)

Unlike the poised dancer, the background buildings subtly convey the notion of imbalance by having a circular window set above one pair of arches and an empty frame over the other.

My wife has been a professional belly dancer for many years and was the inspiration behind the dancer on the card.

The ornate skull smiling on the back of the dancer's belt, as well as all of the metallic trim on her costume, were textured from two pieces of my wife's belly dance jewelry.

Ace of Pentacles

The iron dragon clutches a mystical pentacle with his claws and tail, holding the entire universe in his grip. As he presses the pentacle against his golden chest, it comes alive with energy and opens up a portal into his soul. Through this magical window, one can see the infinite abundance of the cosmos as well as the limitless potential of the dragon's spirit.

The dragon is a creature of pure perfection that is in harmony with both the physical and the spiritual realms. He is also the gatekeeper between humanity and the divine. At present, the pentacle he protects points down towards the ground, indicating that his current concerns lie in the material world. Being the master of his destiny, the dragon has the power to rotate the circular pentacle in whatever direction he wishes.

The card pictures the dragon looking to the viewer's right, suggesting that he focuses heavily on the future. This industrious titan has a clear vision of what he wants from life and will aggressively fight for his fair share. With endless possibilities at hand, the dragon is eager to soar to incredible heights on blood-red wings filled with passion.

Upright meanings:

The powerful Ace of Pentacles symbolizes new financial opportunities and material gain. An epic era of prosperity is about to begin! Now is the perfect time to launch a business venture, start a bold project or seek worthwhile employment. Additionally, a valuable chance to manifest your dreams into reality will suddenly become apparent. Take ferocious action on your ambitions, knowing that you can have it all through hard work and a dedication to excellence. Trust in yourself and find ways to create good fortune. If you do your part to succeed, the universe will happily take care of the rest.

Reversed meanings:

When inverted, the Ace of Pentacles may be a warning that your finances are about to take a turn for the worse. This reversal of fortune might happen because your liabilities have become greater than your assets. Although you seem to make enough money, you often have a hard time holding on to it. At this time, you need to change your loose spending habits. Start saving your cash and do whatever it takes to guard your treasure!

Ace of Coins, rough sketch (2007)

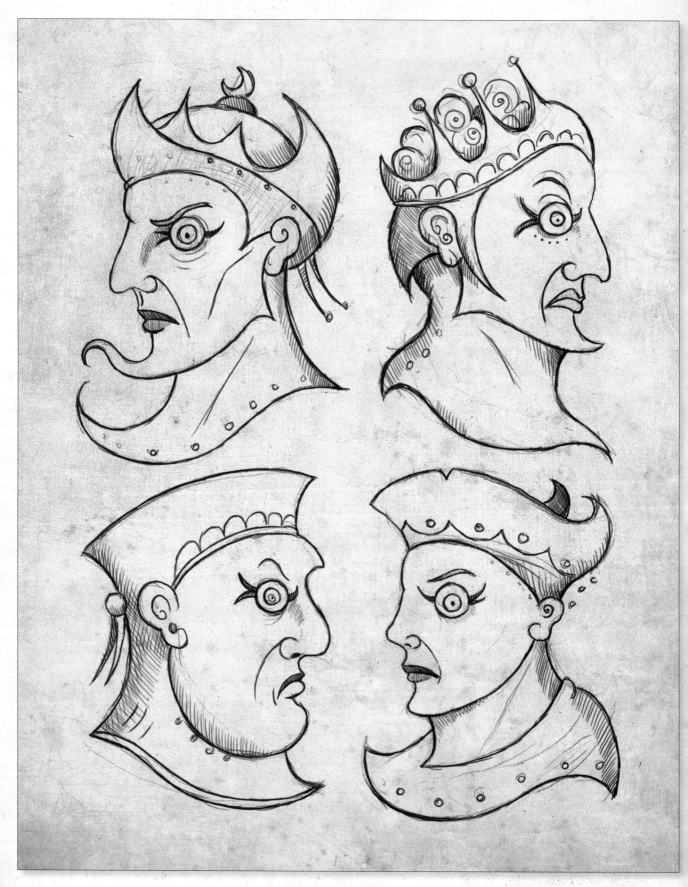

Various coin profile sketches

THE LOST SUIT OF COINS

T he Deviant Moon follows many old tarot traditions. In keeping with early European decks, I originally planned on using coins for the final suit instead of the more modern pentacles. I imagined the coins in a Romanesque style with the profiles of ancient kings and heroes emblazoned on the fronts.

In order to create the Deviant currency, I sculpted over two dozen clay coins. Each one was a half inch thick and the size of a compact disc. After photographing the props, I digitally enhanced the images to give the clay coins a metallic look before inserting them into the cards.

Clay coin props—heads and tails

Experimental silver coin

Experimental silver coin

The Queen's coin before digital enhancement

Clay prop

The Queen presents a monetary donation to her subjects.

The Miser and his money

When I finished creating the suit, I placed some test cards in a row on the wall for evaluation. Each card looked fine individually; however, I felt there was something wrong with the coins when seen all together. As I sat there thinking, my seven-year old daughter, who was always forthright with her critiques, walked into the room and declared that the coins reminded her of cookies! From that moment on, I could only see them as such. It was clear to me now that the coins would bring down the entire deck. Besides, the notion of Deviant citizens hauling colossal currency around never made sense to me, symbolically or otherwise.

In the end, I abandoned the Suit of Coins rather than force the deck to accept something it obviously did not want. After replacing each coin with a uniquely crafted pentacle, I called my daughter in and asked for her opinion. She took a long look at the revised cards and replied, "These are just right! You're all finished!"

With her words, the strange dream I had been working on for over thirty years was finally complete, or so I thought. Little did I realize it was just the beginning.

Five coins embedded in a stained glass window

Eight newly minted coins roll down the conveyer belt.